Hack the
SAT

How to Ace the Most Infamous Test in
the World, with Straight Talk from a
Florida Public School Kid Who Got into
Harvard and Personally Tutored the
American Aristocracy

GOTHAM
BOOKS

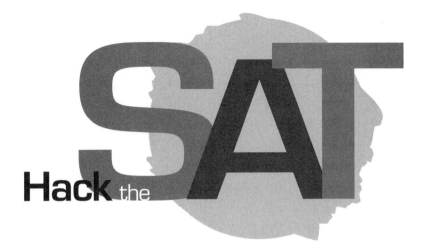

Hack the SAT

A Private SAT Tutor
Spills the Secret Strategies
and Sneaky Shortcuts That
Can Raise Your Score
Hundreds of Points

ELIOT SCHREFER

GOTHAM BOOKS
Published by Penguin Group (USA) Inc.
375 Hudson Street, New York, New York 10014, U.S.A.
Penguin Group (Canada), 90 Eglinton Avenue East, Suite 700, Toronto, Ontario M4P 2Y3, Canada (a division of Pearson Penguin Canada Inc.); Penguin Books Ltd, 80 Strand, London WC2R 0RL, England; Penguin Ireland, 25 St Stephen's Green, Dublin 2, Ireland (a division of Penguin Books Ltd); Penguin Group (Australia), 250 Camberwell Road, Camberwell, Victoria 3124, Australia (a division of Pearson Australia Group Pty Ltd); Penguin Books India Pvt Ltd, 11 Community Centre, Panchsheel Park, New Delhi–110 017, India; Penguin Group (NZ), 67 Apollo Drive, Rosedale, North Shore 0632, New Zealand (a division of Pearson New Zealand Ltd); Penguin Books (South Africa) (Pty) Ltd, 24 Sturdee Avenue, Rosebank, Johannesburg 2196, South Africa

Penguin Books Ltd, Registered Offices: 80 Strand, London WC2R 0RL, England

Published by Gotham Books, a member of Penguin Group (USA) Inc.

First printing, July 2008
10   9   8   7   6   5   4   3   2   1

Library of Congress Cataloging-in-Publication Data
Schrefer, Eliot, 1978–
    Hack the SAT: a private SAT tutor spills the secret strategies and sneaky shortcuts that can raise your score hundreds of points / by Eliot Schrefer.
        p.   cm.
    ISBN 978-1-592-40369-1 (pbk.)
    1. SAT (Educational test)   2. SAT (Educational test)—Study guides.   I. Title.

    LB2353.57.S374 2008
    378.1'662—dc22   2007045993

Printed in the United States of America
Set in Scala
Designed by Susan Hood

For my students, past and present:

Alex, Alexa, Alyssa, Amanda, Amanda, Anais, Anand, Annie, Annie, Ashley, Barry, Ben, Cammy, Caroline, Casey, Claire, Colin, Cosima, Dan, Daniela, David, Dominica, Ed, Eleanor, Eli, Emily, Emma, Erica, Erik, Grace, Hannah, Insia, Isar, Jackie, Jadry, Jen, Jenny, Jeremy, Jessica, Jessica, Jordan, Josh, Josh, Julia, Kate, Kate, Kelsey, Kim, Krysia, Labe, Laura, Lianna, Lindsay, Liz, Luke, Manny, Marina, Marissa, Mark, Marshall, Michael, Michelle, Moishe, Morgan, Nell, Nicholas, Nicole, Nicole, Rachel, Rachel, Rachel, Rachele, Rebecca, Ricky, Robby, Russell, Sam, Sam, Samantha, Schuyler, Scott, Shara, Shira, Sophie, Spencer, Stuart, Susan, Suzi, Sydney, Tassilo, Tory, Valentina, William, Zach, and Zach.

CONTENTS AT A GLANCE

ACTUAL TABLE OF CONTENTS

Part V: Beating the Final Boss 195
(WHAT TO DO WITH EVERYTHING YOU'VE LEARNED, INCLUDING
A PRACTICE DRILL AND APPLICATIONS ADVICE)

INTRODUCTION

Stop Studying So Hard, Dum-Dum

Crack open the giant SAT guides, and it seems like there's a mountain of info to learn. And there *would* be tons to cover—if you hadn't already been going to school for twelve years.

The truth is that the SAT isn't all that overwhelming a test. There's no math on it that you haven't covered in class long ago; the essay is shorter and more forgiving than that of your average final exam; the grammar is just a formalization of language rules you use every time you speak; and the reading passages, while often deadeningly boring, don't require any outside knowledge.

The trick is to adapt what you already know to the test. As far as actual technical learning, *you already know it all.* Just as you've always suspected!

Which isn't to say that you don't still need help.

A few years back some hypercompetitive Manhattan parent realized he could make other kids eat his Suzie's dust by getting her expert help. And so was born the very first private SAT tutor, succeeded through the years by a tight group of brainy Ivy League grads, who carefully cultivated the rules and strategies that would help their students typically gain 375 points or more over a year of tutoring.

Tutoring *works,* with average results far beyond those of a Princeton Review class. We tutors scored in the top percentile, know exactly what it takes to nail the test, and how best to present it.

If getting into college is supposed to be a fair process, then everyone should have access to our little-known strategies. But they don't: the average score among those whose families are in the highest income bracket is 30 percent higher than that of those whose families are in the lowest.

These tricks that have so inflated the scores of those in the know, that cost $40,000 for the year of preparation, have been kept under lock and key. Until now.

Want the same score increases? Read this book.

Who the Hell Is This Schrefer Guy?

Let me introduce you to your new best friend. Me.

I attended a large public high school that had cinderblocks slathered in peach-colored paint, a revered football team, and a population of malcontents that included a small but influential population of nerds. I was one of those nerds, passionately and fully.

We were aware private school kids existed, somewhere, though none of us had ever met any. We figured a cloud of weird feeling would settle over us as soon as we met some. They would be sorta normal, but over-pronounce their Rs. They'd discuss Socrates over (virgin) martinis and maybe have eyes that bugged a little. The guys would wear knotted cardigans and the girls plaid skirts held together with big safety pins.

Well, I ended up going to Harvard, which was full of 'em. My private school friends didn't talk funny (or any funnier than Harvard students generally speak—I swear I heard the word "ubiquitous" daily), or wear plaid skirts unless they were going to a theme party or they were that one girl who wore pearls every day. No, the only thing that made private school kids different was the very fact that they had been to private schools.

Then in 2001 I graduated and landed in New York City (after a great year-long side trip to Rome), trying to make it as a writer and struggling to pay for my milk and bananas and Harlem rent. Like anyone really desperate for cash, I fell back on my best asset. For some people, twenty-two and new to the big city, that means stripping. But my buns aren't so hot; my SAT score was awesome, though, so I started working as a private SAT tutor.

I loved it. The students were generally charming and focused, and those who weren't were all the more interesting. And they all were glad to have a teacher to hang with who talked to them like an equal.

The pay was also pretty darn good. Manhattan tutor rates climb as high as $1,000 an hour. And for what? Access to a set of rules and tips that have been bumping up the scores of America's wealthy for a couple of decades now.

Whether you're in private school or public, whether you live in a yacht with a swimming pool or a trailer with a cesspool, these are the rules you're looking for. Let's crack this nut wide open.

PART I

NINE EPISODES FRoM YoUR JUNIOR YEAR

(Basics of What
You'll Be Facing)

You First Hear About the Test

(or You Experience a Bout of lunchroom Terror)

You're not arriving at the SAT as a blank slate. Perhaps it's because you have an older brother who never got into the University of Guam because of it. Perhaps it's because your parents yak about the test, saying that "no one ever *prepared* back in the day, the world's just gotten so crazy." Perhaps it's because the first day of high school you sat with the juniors by mistake and got an earful of their stress before they inserted you into a trash can. Whatever the cause, you have a whole host of preconceptions. Some are probably right, and some are probably wrong. Let's find out the basics of what we're dealing with before we go any further.

1. The SAT is a three-hour-and-forty-five-minute exam that starts at 8:30 A.M. on a Saturday morning. Once you add in the breaks and set-up it will most likely be 1:30 P.M. by the time you're sitting down to your reward lunch.
2. It has ten sections: three each for Math, Critical Reading, and Writing, and one extra "experimental" section in (randomly) one of the three.
3. The test is offered seven times a year in the United States: October, November, December, January, March/April (varying), May, and June.

ABIDE: TOLERATE

A typical test might break down like this:

Section 1:	Essay	25 minutes
Section 2:	Critical Reading	25 minutes
Section 3:	Math	25 minutes
Section 4:	Math (experimental)	25 minutes
Section 5:	Critical Reading	25 minutes
Section 6:	Math	25 minutes
Section 7:	Grammar	25 minutes
Section 8:	Critical Reading	20 minutes
Section 9:	Math	20 minutes
Section 10:	Grammar	10 minutes

If you're taking the test abroad, check out www.collegeboard.org. You might have fewer available test dates.

4 Scores are out of 2400, 800 for each of Math, Critical Reading, and Writing. Each section is scaled so that 500 is roughly average.

5 Yes, there's an essay. It comes first, lasts twenty-five minutes, and its score is combined with your grammar multiple choice results. But it's nothing to stress about. (More on why later.)

6 You can take the SAT more than once. Although colleges will receive your scores from every test day, they only officially consider your highest score for Math, Critical Reading, and Writing from all the different SATs you took. So yes, that means you *should* take it more than once.

Look at it this way:

Taking the SAT only once is foolish, unless you got between a 2250 and a 2400.

Why Have an Experimental Section, Anyway?

It seems cruel, doesn't it, that the test makers force you to take an extra tenth section. Even more frustrating is that it doesn't count toward your score, but there's no way to know which one it is. *Don't* try to deduce which section to blow off. I once had a student who was sure that a certain section was too odd to be anything but the experimental. He put his head down for the section—and scored 200 points lower than his previous score. Don't be him.

The one thing you can be sure of is that there won't be an experimental essay. Thank God, because that means you'd be writing two.

"Experimental" does, in fact, mean that the test writers are performing experiments on you. They field test questions that they plan to use on later exams. Once they know what percentage of students will get each question right, they can make sure that future SATs are properly balanced.

(Note: if you receive extended time on the SAT because of a learning disability [see page 183], you won't have an experimental section. Which is good, because otherwise you'd be taking the test for, oh, ten days.)

What's Wrong with a Little Score Inflation Among Friends?
(or Why 600 Sounds More Typical Than 500)

The average score on the SAT is around a 1500. Period. Your parents might not think so, your friends might not think so, you might not think so, but it's true. The stats don't lie.

So why does it sound like everyone's scoring higher? For one thing, SAT gossipers are a self-selecting group. Students who find it interesting to talk about their scores are probably scoring well to begin with.

Also, are they showing you actual score reports? Guarantee that a bunch of them are inflating their scores. I see it all the time. Pumping up SAT results is the nerd equivalent of flexing biceps at the community pool.

Taking it twice is ideal.

Taking it three times is also fine—it's an important test, after all.

Taking it four or more times risks making you appear like a test-obsessed freak to colleges. It's time to move on.

What's *not* true about the test:

1. There is no easier test day. Statistics show no marked difference between scores on various administrations.

2. Since scores on each SAT are standardized (aka curved), if a certain test seems especially hard, it will be graded more leniently. So be careful not to judge your scores before you actually receive them.

You Decide to Take the SAT

(OR You Pretend You Have a Choice)

Your new motto:

The SAT is not evil

There's a general tendency to cast the SAT as the wickedest thing to happen to studentkind since gym showers. But hating on the SAT isn't going to do much for your score. The truth is that the SAT, or a test like it, is essential to keeping admissions fair. Before the SAT (and believe it or not there was a time before the SAT), elite colleges couldn't evaluate candidates from far away, so they cheerfully decided not to admit them. That's why Harvard and Yale used to be full of students only from ritzy private schools. So unless you're reading this book on your dorm bed at Exeter, you really shouldn't hate the SAT. It's what gets you into college, after all.

Sure, it's a flawed test. But one exam that has to work for 1.5 million different juniors each year isn't going to be perfect for each one. And sure, it's long, but so were the last five Harry Potters, and look how much fun *those* were. Look at it this way: You wouldn't want your future to rest on a one-hour exam, if that meant missing one question would cost you fifty points. For a test so important, longer is fairer.

ADORN: DECORATE

And the simple truth is that you should at least pretend to agree with me, because people perform much better when they think positively (this goes for schoolwork, relationships, raising puppies, all of it).

Oh boy, the SAT! Yea!

Good thing we've decided we love the SAT, because if you're going to apply to college at all, you're going to have to take it. The only exceptions are if:

You're applying to a community college or to one of the small number of four-year universities that don't require it at all (Bates and Bowdoin are the most famous examples; a complete list is available at www.fairtest.org).

You're applying to a university outside of the United States or Canada. ¡*Felicitaciones*!

You're taking the ACT instead (see page 214).

Your mother is a yellow-throated sparrow (this exemption requires a special waiver from your school counselor).

If none of the above is true, you're stuck with the SAT.

Approach it as a test you've chosen to take, rather than an ordeal that a conspiracy of colleges, parents, and demons is forcing on you (even if that's closer to the truth). People perform better on tasks when two conditions are met: They feel they can affect the outcome, and they feel they've made their own choice to do well.

(Eliot holds for applause.)

Think of it this way: Force your little sister to play with fingerpaints, and she'll do so only as long as you're making her. Let her discover the fingerpaints on her own, and she'll be staining her clothes for hours. View the SAT as your opportunity to show the world your potential. That unmarred test booklet hasn't a single preconception about you, and there's something empowering about that. It won't hold your history of Cs and being late to class against you. All you have to do is prepare the best you can. Which is where this book comes in.

AESTHETIC: RELATING TO BEAUTY

Raw Score	Critical Reading Scaled Score
67	800
66	800
65	800
64	790
63	770
62	750
61	740
60	720
59	710
58	700
57	690
56	680
55	670
54	660
53	650
52	650
51	640
50	630
49	620
48	620
47	610
46	600
45	600
44	590
43	580
42	580
41	570
40	560
39	560
38	550
37	540
36	
35	530
34	520
33	520
32	510

The Bell Curve: Why It's Harder to Raise a 500 Than a 400 or 600

The test makers account for discrepancies in the difficulties of various administrations by tweaking the results so that the typical student always gets around a 500.

Take a look, for example, at this partial scoring breakdown for the Critical Reading portion of a sample SAT. The number on the right is a curved score—i.e., the reported score—while the number on the left is the actual number answered correctly.

If you have a 520, you could get four more questions right and only get a 540. If you were starting at a 710, however, four more questions right would result in a 770. The same concept holds true for the Math and Writing sections.

What does it mean? It means that, if you're in the 500s or low 600s, and your effort means one more question right per practice test, you're going to start slowly and then enjoy a pyrotechnic rise through the upper 600s and 700s. You're still improving just as much, but it will show in the scores much more easily once you're near the top.

As a result, it's easy to become frustrated during the early stages of your preparation, even if you're making steady progress. Just slog through the doldrums of the 500s and low 600s, and you'll see it all pay off later.

AGGRAVATE: WORSEN

You Choose Test Dates

(OR You Realize That Test Dates Are Far Less Fun Than Real Dates)

The classic little black dress SAT date is May. That's when the biggest swarm of high school juniors throngs the test centers, causing retired English teachers across the country to go blind and batty reading mile-high piles of essays on "the virtues of leadership," or similar rubbish.

There's good reason everyone aims for the May administration. Without even trying, you'll get wiser and more mature throughout your junior year (a good 10–30 points wiser, based on my experience). Also, it gives you more time to pore over this book.

The typical student will take the SAT in May, the subject tests in June (more on those in a sec), and retake either one in October.

If you're a high scorer (above 1800), you'll want to plan on taking the SAT more often, starting in January or March. You can expect big score differences between test administrations, and may need to take the SAT a few times to get your highest result. Same goes for very low scorers (under 1300).

Here's why: Typical students, who are scoring in the 400–600 range on their sections, aren't going to have scores that move much, because they're at the center of the bell curve. Scores at the center are statistically far more sluggish—getting one more math question right at 500 might

Register as early as you can for your SAT. The official registration deadline is always approximately five weeks before the test date, but if you register early you'll have a better chance of scoring a good test location. I've had students who had to cross state lines to take their SAT because they registered late. So go online and do it now.

If the SAT is tomorrow and you've forgotten to register, don't panic. Test centers offer stand-by testing (for an extra fee, of course). The test makers mail many more test booklets than they have registered students, in order to soak up cash from walk-ins. They print so many, in fact, that in all my years of tutoring *I've never had a stand-by student turned away*. There's some risk involved, of course, so you're better off registering. To play it safe, if you must take the SAT stand-by, choose a test center that's a larger facility; they're more likely to have the space to fit you in.

not change the score at all, while that same question right can raise a 760 to a 790. (For more details, see the box on page 9.)

You can retake the SAT or Subject Tests in November, December, or maybe even January of your senior year, if you need to. October's just the last date that's sure to meet early application deadlines. Take the test any later and you'll have to confirm with the colleges you're applying to that you're not going to be too late.

You Realize That There Are SAT Subject Tests

(or You Say, "These, Too?!&#!")*

In a deadly blow to the social lives of high school juniors and seniors everywhere, somewhere along the way the test makers decided to compel students to take not just one SAT but *four*. Yes, it was the birth of the Subject Tests*, a series of virtually obligatory hour-long tests that cover topics ranging from the sciences to math to literature to foreign language.

The Subject Tests take an already fraught process and make it super-stressful. The confusion of planning for them is enough to make your dad yell "this is crazy" and rip the calendar into pieces, and tell you to take care of it yourself. At least that's how it worked in my house.

Though you have to take more of them, the Subject Tests should weigh less in your mind than the SAT, for a couple of reasons:

1 They don't matter as much in college admissions.
2 They're a lot more straightforward.

If you're preparing for any Advanced Placement exams, you'll find the questions on the Subject Tests much like those multiple choice

*Not to be confused with the SSAT (which is taken for admission to private high schools).

questions. Hard, sure, but not *sneaky* like the SAT. Many colleges require you to take three of them, some only two, and still others none at all. You'll want to check the admissions brochures for the schools you're interested in, and schedule your tests accordingly. It's smart to take your subject tests in June, when you'll already be studying for similar final exams. (If you've already crammed for your Italian final, you might as well get the Italian Subject Test out of the way at the same time.) You'll get your scores over the summer and can decide whether to use the October test to retake the SAT or Subject Tests or (lucky duck) not retake anything at all.

Now, which tests to take? There's a piece of tutor wisdom that suggests taking Subject Tests in fields that will bolster weaker areas of your transcript. If you got a low grade in precalculus you should try to nail the Math II test, for example. Sounds good, but then again it's also really hard to ace material that you didn't do well on the first time it came around.

What your Subject Tests are really about is pure numbers. Register for the tests that will give you the highest scores, period. The College Board publishes a book called *The Official Study Guide for All SAT Subject Tests* (it should be in your local library), which contains one copy of each

Sophomores Taking Subject Tests? WTF?

You might hear of sophomores registering for subject tests. It's generally a bad idea, as you're simply a better test taker once you're a junior and have another year of coursework under your belt. There's one exception, however: *science* tests. If you take a biology class in sophomore year, for example, and don't plan on taking one ever again, you might as well take the Subject Test sophomore year and be done with it. Then you've got a test down, and can worry about one less in junior year. Outside of the sciences, there's really no other case in which it's called for, however.

Subject Test. Pick four or five tests out, and take a practice exam in each. Once June comes around, sit the tests that correspond to your highest scores.

As you tackle your practice Subject Tests, try not to get nervous. They're all hard, but they also have very generous curves, much kinder, even, than the SAT. You can leave fifteen questions out of ninety-five blank on the World History test, for example, and still get a perfect score. And getting just half right is a 600, well above the national average. So even if you feel terrible about yourself while you're taking the Subject Tests, you might be pleasantly surprised when you see your results.

Here's advice about each of the most popular subject tests:

Math I/II

The biggies. Many colleges will require you to take either the Math I or II Subject Test to apply.

But which one to choose?

The content of the II is definitely more advanced. While trigonometry comprises only 6 percent of the I, it's more like 26 percent of the II. If you've gotten substantially into trigonometry, analytic geometry, or precalculus coursework, then you'll be in good shape for the II.

There are other good reasons to opt for the level II. Because it's a tougher test, the curve is better. While you can leave seven questions blank on a typical II and still get a perfect score, you can't miss any on a I and get a perfect score. The II has a double advantage, then: It's more impressive to colleges and, because of the curve, might wind up being a higher score anyway. The only case in which you wouldn't want to consider the II is if you haven't taken any pre-calculus. Again, sit yourself down with *The Official Study Guide for All SAT Subject Tests* and

AMORPHOUS: SHAPELESS

see how you score on the two tests. If your II is within 20–30 points of your I score, or better, then go for the II.

When you're stuck on a problem, be sure to make full use of your graphing calculator. If you're asked how many times a trigonometric function will hit the *x*-axis, for instance, graphing is a foolproof solution.

Our most important SAT math strategy, plugging in numbers (see page 82), is also invaluable on the math Subject Tests.

History

Two history tests are offered: United States History and World History. Expect to take huge casualties on either test, but the curve is extremely kind. Answering just over half of the U.S. questions and leaving the remainder blank would net you a perfectly respectable 600 (and yes, that means the typical student gets fewer than half right).

United States: There's a lot of overlap with the AP exam. If you take the Subject Test in the same spring as a U.S. AP, you'll cut down massively on your study time.

World: Fewer students take the World History test, and that's because few high schools offer a world history course in the junior or senior year, and so most students assume they're unequipped. But don't shy away from this test just because you're not taking a world history course at the moment. Since the test is so hilariously broad (it covers a couple more millennia and five more continents than the U.S. exam), the questions feel more like trivia. If you're an ace at *Jeopardy!*, give World History a shot. Again, start by taking a practice test and seeing how you score.

ANECDOTE: STORY

Note: Glance over the major periods of art history, which you might not have ever covered in school. Hit your school library or Wikipedia.

The Sciences

(CHEMISTRY, PHYSICS, BIOLOGY)

Each of these tests can be tough. Most of my students avoid them, unless they fall into one of two categories:

1. They are science geeks. If you're wondering whether you are one, too, then you're not. (Quick test: Do you know the first and last names of all the characters in *Battlestar Galactica*?)
2. They are taking a science course that will finish at the same time as they take the Subject Test.

Foreign Language

(CHINESE, FRENCH, GERMAN, HEBREW, ITALIAN, JAPANESE, KOREAN, LATIN, SPANISH)

It's easy to get a decent score on a foreign language Subject Test, but hard to get a very high one. High school students tend to fall into one of two categories: They either speak a foreign language natively, or couldn't order a Coke abroad. For that reason, there are plenty of people who will bomb a Subject Test in a foreign language, and just as many who will ace it. Therefore, if you're a good student but not especially savvy at languages, expect a score that's fine, but not great.

Two further notes:

Since no one's a native speaker of Latin (you can't speak Latin, yo), that test should be easier . . . but it's not. It's notoriously hard, because the pool of test takers is skewed toward hard-core students.

Proportionally, the Asian languages have more native speakers taking them. Only choose one of them if you've studied really hard. Or if your mother was singing to you in Korean as she changed your diapers.

Literature

Literature is another nicely curved test, and a popular choice for students who don't want to prepare much. You need to know some basic terms of literary analysis (sonnet, personification, meter, etc.), but otherwise there's not too much preparation necessary. You don't need to know any specific authors or texts. All you have to do is to be able to make it through various passages and answer questions about what you've read—it's glorified reading comprehension. Just follow the same guidelines for reading passages set out in this book.

The test makers don't release many copies of the Literature test, because they reuse them with some frequency. Some administrations are infamously hard, and others are comparatively easy. If you're going to take the Literature test, keep this fact in mind and steel yourself to retake it in case you're randomly assigned a harder test.

Note: The questions on the Literature test are very similar to the multiple choice questions on the AP English Language and Literature exams, though the passages are shorter.

Spotted on the Job, Posh 5th Avenue Penthouse:

Wrinkled poster of Josh Hartnett set into an ornately gilt eighteenth-century frame.

You Come Up with a Preparation Plan

(OR You Have Your Secretary Clear Your Social Calendar for the Next Year)

There are a few options for how to use this book:

1. **Minimal potential:** Buy it just to get your parents off your back. Promptly discard.
2. **Medium potential:** Read it cover to cover and enjoy the few dozen extra points it will help you scrape off the test.
3. **Maximum potential:** Read it and then practice. Private tutoring works so well because my students take practice tests. Lots of practice tests—optimally, around a dozen. This book will give you the foreknowledge to help you get the most out of your practice tests. Think of it as your SparkNotes to the *Moll Flanders* of the SAT.

Read this book through, then go take a swim. Between each lap, tell yourself: "I'm going to take a practice test every Saturday morning until the SAT arrives."

Great. Now you'll need to get your hands on some practice tests. The big old Princeton Review and Kaplan books are adequate but not

ARCANE: MYSTERIOUS

I Stand for Nothing: A History of the SAT's Name

When the SAT was introduced in 1901, it was announced as the Scholastic Achievement Test. It was renamed in 1941 to the Scholastic Aptitude Test, to reflect a shift from measuring academic success to the *potential* for success (i.e., intelligence). In 1990, because of uncertainty about the test's ability to determine intelligence, the name shifted again to the Scholastic Assessment Test. Finally, in 1994, the College Board declared that the initials *didn't stand for anything*, largely to defuse expectations that the test could measure any one thing.

That's right. All this preparation for a test that officially doesn't stand for anything.

But consider this: In 2002, back when the test was out of 1600, the average combined Math and Verbal score for those whose families earned less than $10,000 was 859. For those whose families earned more than $100,000 a year, it was 1123.

As one of my students suggested, perhaps it should really be called the Scholastic Affluence Test.

(If you didn't get the joke, go study your vocab.)

excellent; both companies have spent years honing their test-writing abilities, and as a result have come up with some breathtakingly mediocre practice tests. Much better is *The Official SAT Study Guide* ($19.95). You'll be working with real questions from genuine SATs, and there's no better way to prepare yourself than that. Once you've worked through all those, click to www.collegeboard.org and look into the "Official SAT Online Course." It offers six more practice tests, in addition to the one free test that's available to anyone. I'd suggest you get at least nine other friends to chip in for the membership, which lowers the cost from $70 to $7 each. You can call yourselves the Sisterhood of the Traveling SATs, or something less dorky.

The Man's out to empty your wallet. Just get *The Official SAT Study Guide* from the library—your school's bound to have a bunch of copies.

AUGMENT: INCREASE

Between the book and the online course, you'll have access to fifteen practice tests, more than enough for you to get yourself into top SAT-fighting shape.

So, to summarize:

1. Read this book.
2. Take a practice test each week, flipping through this book beforehand.
3. Nail your SAT.

Done.

Easy Tear-out Study Schedules

(For your bulletin board or mirror. Bedroom use only; don't tape SAT schedules on your locker door or you will get beaten up.)

- -

If You're Starting a Year Before the Test

Go relax for three months and come see me then.

- -

If You're Starting Nine Months Before the Test

(Typically, beginning early in junior year and working through to the May test.)

September:

1. Take a full practice test under real conditions, one weekend morning. (Download one free from collegeboard.org, kaplan.com, or review.com.)
2. Begin studying this book.

October–December:

1. Now is when you'll be doing most of your up-front work. You should learn all the vocab running along these pages, study a few sections each week, and do the drills, making sure you really have them all down.

BANAL: DULL

2 Right when winter break begins, take another full-length practice test. If your score's gone up, great—but don't worry if it hasn't. That's very typical. December is a month of anxious phone calls to tutors, because it seems like all the work isn't paying off yet—but it will. Typically your scores will only start to rise after three or more practice tests.

January–May:

1 Take a practice exam every weekend that you can. I'd love for you to try at least ten. Take any problems you just can't figure out to a parent (which usually won't lead anywhere) or a teacher. Occasionally try to take your practice tests in unfamiliar environments, like the school library or a parent's office.

2 Continue to study vocab.

3 At some point in April, go to kaplan.com and register for a free administered SAT. It's important that you take at least one exam in a more accurate environment before you go in for the real thing.

If You're Starting Three Months Before the Test

You can still get a lot done.

1 Take a diagnostic test on your own.

2 Spend a month working through this book a few times over.

3 Administer yourself practice tests once a week for the last two months. I'd like you to take at least six.

4 Take a free test (as above) shortly before your real SAT.

BELIE: CONTRADICT

If You're Starting One Month Before the Test

You can still get a lot done.

1. Take a diagnostic test on your own.
2. Spend a weekend skimming through this book.
3. Take at least two practice tests.
4. Skim through the book again. Read all the vocab words, even if you haven't memorized them.
5. Take a free test (as above) shortly before your real exam.

If You're Starting One Week Before the Test

Repeat after me (frantically): I can still get a lot done.

1. Take a diagnostic test (as above).
2. Spend a day skimming through this book.
3. Take another exam.

If You're Starting the Night Before the Test

Inscribe "I can still get a lot done" onto your forearm with a Bic pen. Order a pizza.

1. Read this book throughly, being sure at least to do the drills.
2. Watch the first season of your favorite show on DVD.
3. Pray if you are so inclined.

BENEVOLENT: GOOD

You Take the PSAT

(OR You Hit the Speed Bump That Wrecks Your Suspension)

Don't freak out about the PSAT.

For those of you who have been homeschooled in Tahiti or have had your memory banks overfilled by Facebook profiles, the PSAT is a free practice SAT that's administered in the fall, generally in your own school, during the week or on a Saturday (your school's choice—if it's during the week, you get to miss class—bonus).

The dirty secret is that the PSAT doesn't matter much. It becomes an obsession because everyone in your school takes it at once, and therefore fixates on it, like any group will do about common experiences. To your parents, that tri-color PSAT score report (which arrives around mid-December, FYI) will seem critically important. That's because it's their first sense of what your standardized test—and therefore, college—prospects will be. But rip out this mini-card and give it to them:

The College Board is big on claiming that the PSAT is an essential way to familiarize yourself with the SAT and to figure out where you stand before you take the real thing. That's definitely true, but cynics will observe that it's also a perfect way to panic students just in time for them to buy scads of College Board prep books and online programs—which, at prices of $19.99 to $69.99, make the College Board a bundle.

Dear Mom and Dad:
Sure, you can get legitimately nervous about the SAT. But
please try as much as you can to forget about the PSAT.
My scores don't count, and . . .
They're not very accurate anyway.
Love,
Your Kid

As part of their massive funds devoted to research, the test makers
have studied just how lengthy to make the SAT so that scores are stable
and predictable. If the SAT were only one question long, you'd get either
the top score or the lowest score, and even a chicken with a number two
pencil glued to its beak could luck into a 2400. The SAT tops three and a
half hours for a reason.

The PSAT lasts just over two hours, which means it's less accurate.
When you get those numbers back, remember that they're only ball park.
Your actual SAT score might be significantly higher or lower—so don't
get gloomy or arrogant.

Even beyond questions of accuracy, the PSAT doesn't really matter. The
only people who will see your results are you, your parents (if your score
sheet doesn't "get lost on the way home"), and your guidance counselor
(if she's like mine was, she won't pay it any more attention than to spill a
bottle of nail polish on it).

Colleges can't access your scores. If Paradise College wants to send
admissions material to kids within a certain range of PSAT scores, they'll
pay for a list of those students. But they won't know your specific results.
So don't worry.

You may have heard about scholarships based on PSAT scores, most
famously the National Merit Scholarship. It earns you $2,500, and is
based almost exclusively on a ranking derived from your PSAT score.
That $2,500 is cool, sure, but compared to the amounts of college
tuitions, it's a drop in the bucket. The scholarship is prestigious, and

BOORISH/BRUSQUE/IMPUDENT/CURT: RUDE

The "Non-profit" ETS

The College Board is officially a non-profit. But that doesn't make them nearly as altruistic as the name might suggest. All it means is that the College Board doesn't have shareholders, and that their financial accountings must be available to the public. That didn't stop them from netting $30 million in profits in a recent year (2003).

And the Educational Testing Service, which actually manufactures the test for the College Board, is no better. The top eight ETS officials pull in over $300,000 a year each, with the president making way over $700,000. While the ETS Web site front page defensively proclaims that "at non-profit ETS, our sole mission is to advance learning," their finances tell another story.

So, if you're feeling gooey for ETS and its benevolent efforts to help students get to college, you can check it. The SATs are a business, and your $41.50 to take the exam is helping line their wallets. The College Board is in the business of both test administration and test prep. If that seems inherently unfair, it should—it's like a doctor whacking your knee with a sledgehammer and then offering to patch you up. Thanks Doc!

would certainly be a huge boost to your college application . . . but you only find out about it long after you've already gotten into school. So it's useless.

Treat the PSAT as what it's officially meant to be—a way to get some early experience with the SAT. Don't go overboard preparing for it.

You Discover Which Questions to Skip

(or You Meet the Best Question You Never Answered)

You've probably heard that you get penalized for guessing on the SAT.

What does that mean?

What it *doesn't* mean is that some teacher is watching you and making a note in a special column whenever you glance about the room and helplessly tap your pencil on your lips before marking your answer.

It also doesn't mean that guessing is always a bad idea.

Basically, the test makers want to make sure that no one can Christmas tree a test and luck her way into a good score. To do so, they came up with the diabolical idea of *deducting* a quarter point for every wrong answer, making you worse off than if you just left the question blank. If you turned in your SAT without a single mark, you'd get around a 230 on each section. If you actually got every problem wrong, you could go as low as 200.

Let's give a five-question quiz to two hapless students, Biff and Buff. As Buff has somehow misplaced his arms, he has no choice but to leave his test blank. Biff, having the advantage of being able to hold a pencil, guesses randomly.

"To Christmas tree" a test means to fill in bubbles as if randomly placing ornaments on a tree.

Don't Freak over Three in a Row

I've observed a definite temptation to overanalyze the letters you're putting on your answer sheet.

You get three E's in a row, for example, or answers 13–19 spell out "D E A D D A D," so you run from the room and call home.

Stop. Don't change answers because you came up with some harebrained theory that you should never have three of the same letters in a row. That's just dumb. There have been SATs on which the same letter appeared *four* times in a row. So don't freak out and change answers. Superstition is no reason to mess everything up.

And no, C doesn't occur more often than any other letter.

Buff would get a zero; that much is certain. But Biff would be bound to get one of the five correct, probability says. Which means one point, woo hoo! But count how many he *missed,* which would be four and take off a quarter point for each, and suddenly he's back at zero, just as if he'd answered no questions at all.

Now let's say Biff got some elementary education, and so he is able to eliminate one answer choice for each question, and will guess among the rest. This time, he'll have a one in four chance of getting each question right, which means he would likely get as many as two right. Taking away a quarter point for each missed problem, he would get $2 - \frac{3}{4} = 1\frac{1}{4}$ points. Which is better than nothing!

If you just broke into a rash because I threw statistics at you without any warning, don't sweat the figures. Just remember: *If you have no clue on a problem, there's no point in guessing. But if you can eliminate even one answer choice, then it's in your best interest to guess.*

Let's take it a step further: Once you've read this book and taken at least one practice test, you'll have developed a gut sense for which answer choices are less likely to be correct. Unless you haven't had time to take even a first look at a question, you'll want to put some answer down.

An exception to this "always guess" rule is if you're scoring lower than 450 on your sections. In that case spend your time on the early (easy) questions, and allow yourself to skip any and all hard questions.

CALLOW: IMMATURE

You Hear About the Perfect Score That You'll Never Get

(Or You Learn Not to Say, "I'll Show You Mine if You Show Me Yours")

Not talking about your SAT score, like confidently turning down a cigarette at a party, can actually make you rise in people's estimation. All of a sudden everyone else's maniacal score-squabbling (and frantic trips to the 7-Eleven for Marlboros) will seem lame, and you'll sail above it all serenely.

Only, of course, if you pull it off right.

What you can't do is chat about your potential SAT score all the weeks leading in, publicly wonder about when the results will finally come, then be surprised by a low score and declare that you were above gossiping in the first place. So here's your plan:

Random Social Note: When you're hanging out in a group, people aren't evaluating you nearly as much as you think.

1. A couple of weeks before the test, announce that you've decided to impose a moratorium on SAT talk. People will go along with it, because all of a sudden it will feel lame to have been fixating on a standardized test in the first place.

2. Get your scores.

3a. If the scores aren't worth blabbering about, then you've already declared that you weren't going to say anything about them. No one will suspect you're hiding something.

3b. If your scores turn out to be great, then you have two more options:

4a. Blab about them every-where. Rename your MySpace page after your SAT score.

4b. Continue to take the high road. If you scored higher than most of your friends, it will feel awesome at first to let them know. But you'll also be aware that you're cashing in on some-one else's bad feeling, and that will backfire. (People rarely take to a classmate who is better than them, unless that person pretends she isn't.)

You Get Ready to Take the Test Again

*(OR Your Tutor Tells You,
"Sorry Bud, Time to Retake")*

To get through all of this standardized testing without lasting emotional scars, resign yourself to retaking the SAT before you even sit it the first time.

It's an important test. Even if you do fine the first time, do you want to base your next four years on a "fine" result? Unless you outperform your expectations, plan on taking the SAT a second time.

For one, colleges compile your highest scores on each section *from multiple administrations*. That means they'll take, say, your Math score from March, your Critical Reading score from May, and your Writing score from October to come up with the best combination of the three. (They're not just being nice! It's in a college's best interest to compile your highest scores, because that improves the profile of their entering class in the all-important *U.S. News & World Report* rankings.)

That said, colleges will have access to all of your scores, not just the highest. It would be naive to think that, if they have two equally matched candidates, they won't eventually take a look at your lower scores. This fact means that if you do fine on Critical Reading and Writing in May, say, and want to raise your Math for October, don't concentrate *solely* on Math. While it's okay if your scores on the Critical Reading and Writing fall a bit, you don't want them to plummet.

PART II

CRITICAL
READING

(Cheap Tricks from
Your Tutor, with
Commentary from
Various Sassy Students)

If your SAT were an action movie, the Critical Reading sections would be when everything slows down a little because the hero inexplicably gets involved in a side romance. You know, like when the pretty D.A. pulls him to one side before they sprint across the burning bridge, just to say that she's hoping to survive long enough to visit her sick father in the hospital, and that, she doesn't know what, that she . . . and the hero kisses her. That kind of stuff.

That's reading comprehension for you. Eye-numbingly boring.

Your Tutor Explains It All for You (and Finds Love Along the Way)

You know how some people have a gift? Like for knowing what their friends are thinking, or helping the poor, or picking only the whole Doritos out of the bag?

No one has a gift for Critical Reading.

Sure, plenty of people have a gift for reading. Plenty of people have a gift for being critical (most of my exes, for example). But no one is particularly natural at *critical reading*, this seemingly endless stuff that jams the SAT full of tiny blue print and passages about the subtle revelations of medieval scientist nuns.

The reason no one's totally at home with Critical Reading is that the process is so counterintuitive. The directions ask you to analyze passages, but then the questions require you to summarize them instead (two very different concepts, as we'll get into shortly). Your vocab is tested in unnatural ways (how many times in your writing life will you face a preconstructed sentence with blanks in it?). Both genius-level and subpar thinkers will be stumped on questions that mediocre students sail right through, for reasons we'll also soon discuss.

What does all this mean? It means that even those students who get high scores on Critical Reading find it more draining than the Math or Grammar sections. While each Math question is a fresh puzzle, in Critical Reading you'll have to answer ten questions about the same topic. Your brain will become sluggish under the weight of all the information you're taking in. It's the most exhausting of the sections, for sure. (Pray for a Math or Grammar experimental section.)

CASTIGATE: SCOLD

Many Critical Reading questions have a number of answer choices that seem equally valid (though I'll teach you how to sort through even those). And chances are, you're going to come across vocab words you've never seen. Try not to sweat it too much. Critical Reading is the most frustrating of the SAT's three sections for almost all of my students. You're not alone if you think it's hard.

Just because it's hard doesn't mean that you're necessarily going to score any worse. Critical Reading's actually got the kindest curve of all three sections. Leave three questions blank on Critical Reading and you've still got a 790; do the same on Math and you've got a 740. And remember: Since everyone finds it hard, your score might be higher than you expect, thanks to the curve.

critical reading is so hot.

Used to be that the Critical Reading section (formerly known as "Verbal") was more complex. Until 2005, it included a bunch of analogies, which were very vocabulary intensive. Now, it's down to two question types: Each Critical Reading section will

Don't Expect the Same Percentage Right as a Test in H.S.

A lot of students are way too hard on themselves when they first take a practice SAT. Someone might look over a section he just completed and think, "Hmm . . . I can't have gotten more than half right. I just failed the effing SAT." If he had been taking a final exam, 50 percent would indeed have been an F. But on the SAT, it's an average score. That's right. On a typical SAT, if you answered half of the questions right on each section and left the rest blank (factoring out the essay), you'd have a 520 on Critical Reading, a 520 on Math, and a 500 on Writing. All actually above (or right around, in the case of Writing) the national average.

Seventy-five percent right? Not a C by any stretch. A 630 Critical Reading, a 640 Math, and a 620 on Writing. Not bad at all.

So cut yourself some slack. The SAT is harder than a test you take in school. And the curve reflects it.

CAUSTIC: CORROSIVE

begin with a page of sentence completions, then move on to reading passages.

Although you'll get the occasional "vocabulary in context" question on your reading passages, your biggest test of vocab will be in the sentence completions.

If you have an older sibling who prepared for the SAT before 2005, or if your parents have a good memory, you've probably gotten an earful about how important it is to study vocabulary. Though it's still important, it's only half as important as it was on the old test. Truth is, you can scrape by without knowing a lot of big words; before, it would have been bad news. So while I still want you to study the words at the bottom of this book's pages, you don't have to be a maniac about them.

If you do like to read, then you're in luck. But maybe you don't. Here's the test. Open your Web browser and click the little arrow to see your recently visited pages. Is SparkNotes.com on there? Gotcha.

But that's not to say there's no way around it. I've had plenty of students who've nailed the SAT Critical Reading section even though they've always chosen *Jane* magazine over *Jane Eyre*.

You'll just have to be more wily.

Um, what's *Jane* magazine?

CENSOR: EDIT

Learning Pretty Words

It might seem random for the SAT to test vocabulary—sure, words are important and all, but is measuring how many pretentious terms you know *really* the best way to measure how prepared you are for college? (Snort.)

The brutal answer, Mr. Cynic, is yes. The people who make the SAT love to undertake research projects (part of where your $41.50 test fee is going), and have studied correlations between SATs and college performance. On the Verbal section, the strongest predictor of good college grades is vocabulary. It's flat-out the best way to gauge how much you've read. And students who read a lot tend to be (big surprise) more college-prepared than those who don't.

Which isn't to say you're doomed if the most advanced materials you've read are *Charlie and the Chocolate Factory* and half an issue of *Seventeen*. You're in luck, for three reasons. First, aren't the relationship quizzes fun? Second, the new SAT doesn't test vocabulary nearly as much as the old one did. Third, the test makers are oddly lazy about the words they choose, and test the same vocabulary over and over. So check out the words running along these pages—there's a good chance you'll be seeing them again, if you know what I mean.

These words, by the way, haven't been chosen arbitrarily. I've included them because they've appeared frequently on SATs in the 1990s and 2000s. If there's one thing the SAT makers are famous for, it's reusing words. If you know all the vocab in this book, you'll have seen most of what'll be on your test. It's more than a vocab list—it's a cheat sheet.

CHIMERICAL: FANCIFUL

If you have a few months left before the exam, try actually reading the novels you're assigned in English, instead of diving straight into the SparkNotes. Or get your parents to buy you a subscription to *Vanity Fair*, which has elevated vocabulary and also some damn sexy photos.

Sentence Completions: Why Never Having Read a Book in Your Life Will Bite You in the Ass (and a Few Ways to Fake It)

Sentence completions are simple fill-in-the-blank questions. For example:

My critical reading score will be, without a doubt, -------.
   a. ostentatious   **d. slimy**
   b. infamous   **e. purple**
   c. frickin' awesome

This question's facetious, so I'll let you decide the answer on this one. If you put D or E, send me an e-mail and let me know how. I'm curious.

There are only two rules to remember on sentence completion questions.

RULE #1: *Put Your Own Word in the Blank Before You Even Glance at the Answer Choices*

There's a good reason for this one. The question writers will sneakily offer you words in the answer choices that start to *sound* right, even though they're wrong. If you're planning on just tripping along and reading the sentence with each answer choice until one sounds right, you're asking to get screwed.

CIRCUMVENT: GO AROUND (**CIRCUM**FERENCE = PERIMETER OF A CIRCLE)

Ex. **Even though we all thought of Tim as very athletic, the coach didn't have him run in the district competition, opting instead for someone who was even more ----------.**

    a. fit   d. available

    b. incongruous   e. obsequious

    c. popular

> **Note: All examples in this book are directly adapted from real SAT questions.**

If we just try the answer choices, fit seems good, but then . . . why not popular? The coach could want someone who is likeable. Or why not available? The coach would go for someone who was sure to be around. Or why not the long words? They sound smarter. Here's where Critical Reading gets tricky. It's so easy to second-guess yourself, unless you train yourself otherwise.

Here's the optimal way to solve a problem like this one:

We'd put our own word in the blank. At least while you're beginning, go as far as to even pencil it in. The clearest word for the blank would be "athletic."

Even though we all thought of Tim as very athletic, the coach didn't have him run in the district competition, opting instead for someone who was even more <u>athletic</u>.

Good. Now that we've written that down, ignore the rest of the sentence. We just want to see

Occurred on the Job, Englewood, New Jersey:

Black car sent to pick up tutor in Manhattan and deliver him to New Jersey to work with daughter of "businessman." Tutor to this day convinced he was working for mob.

which word best matches "athletic." And that would definitely be "fit," choice **A**.

Let's try this approach again:

$\mathcal{E} x$. **Mrs. Lohan ran to her daughter's aid and fought off the marauding paparazzi, saving her child from her ‑‑‑‑‑‑‑‑‑‑‑.**

Before I even show you the answer choices, let's come up with our own word. "Um, something bad was going to happen to Lindsay. Uh . . ." Don't worry about it sounding elegant. Just pick something. "Okay. Badness. Saving her child from her badness."

Mrs. Lohan ran to her daughter's aid and fought off the marauding paparazzi, saving her child from her <u>badness</u>.

Now let's look at the answer choices and see which one best matches "badness."

a. benevolence   d. altruism
b. anticipation   e. plight
c. tenacity

Aww! Go, Mrs. Lohan!

Some of you will instantly see choice **E** as the right answer. But say you don't know the word "plight." Let's go by *process of elimination*, which is the best way to solve all Critical Reading problems, both sentence completions and reading passages. Benevolence means something good, so A's out (the root "ben" always means good, like "bueno" in Spanish and "bien" in French). Anticipation isn't badness, and neither is altruism, so there go B and D. And "tenacity" . . . say we're not sure what it means, but it doesn't sound like a terrible thing.

Even if you were totally split between C and E, you'd want to pick one. As long as you're able to eliminate even one answer choice, guess (for a refresher on guessing strategies, see pages 29–30).

Let's try another:

Ex. **Some people argue that video games, with their in-depth characterizations and cinematic sequences, have recently come to resemble films; true fanatics, however, point out that even back when technology was far more ----------, the best video games still had compelling story lines.**

  a. evolved   **d. integral**

  b. rudimentary   **e. lauded**

  c. innocuous

geek!

So, first we fill in the blank with our own word . . . hmm . . . let's read the sentence a couple of times first. It appears to say that while some critics think video games have only recently gotten movielike, others say that they were movielike even back when they had lame graphics. That was back when technology was more . . . basic. So our word is "basic."

Let's ignore the sentence now, and just match "basic" to the answer choices. Cross off what you can, and then guess among the remaining options.

The correct option is **B**, rudimentary. "Evolved" means advanced, "innocuous" means harmless, "integral" means essential, and "lauded" means praised.

Again, our strategy to put our own word in the blank is essential, since if you just started examining the answer choices, you could place a word like "lauded" into the blank and talk yourself into thinking that technology might have once been more praised than it is now. But that's not the *definitional* choice for the blank. We only want the choice whose meaning can be derived from elsewhere in the sentence, and the idea of praise doesn't occur elsewhere.

Just under half of the sentence completion questions will have two blanks:

Ex. **The attendees of Duchess Ashwina's birthday party were delighted to find that, far from being the ----------- affair they had imagined, the festivities were extraordinarily -----------.**

> **a. grim / antiquated** **d. lavish / merry**
>
> **b. foreign / mundane** **e. lugubrious / resourceful**
>
> **c. somber / mirthful**

The attendees were "delighted," so it must have been a great party. Let's put "great" in the second blank, then. For the first blank, we want the opposite of "great," since it's what the festival was "far from." How about "bad." Now the sentence looks like:

> **The attendees of Duchess Ashwina's birthday party were delighted to find that, far from being the <u>bad</u> affair they had imagined, the festivities were extraordinarily <u>great</u>.**

Really inelegant sentence, but it gets the job done.

COLLUDE: CONSPIRE

RULE #2: *When a Sentence Completion Has Two Blanks, Start By Matching the Second Blank First*

The test writers intentionally make many of the first blank words work, because they know most students will (logically) start there. We can save time by starting with the second blank. Which of the words in the second position means "good"?

If you're like most students, you'd say definitely D, and maybe C and E (C because you're not sure what it means, E because it's a positive thing, even if you're not sure about how it works here). So cross out A and B.

Now let's consider the first blank. Don't forget, we're only considering C, D, and E now. Which has a first word that means "bad"?

Definitely not D, "lavish." C, "somber," could work, and maybe E, "lugubrious," works. So we're down to two choices, C and E.

You have a couple of options at this point. If you have no clue, you could guess. You have a 50 percent shot, which isn't bad at all. Or you can finally plug your answers into the sentence and see how it reads:

[C]: The attendees of Duchess Ashwina's birthday party were delighted to find that, far from being the <u>somber</u> affair they had imagined, the festivities were extraordinarily <u>mirthful</u>.

[E]: The attendees of Duchess Ashwina's birthday party were delighted to find that, far from being the <u>lugubrious</u> affair they had imagined, the festivities were extraordinarily <u>resourceful</u>.

Even if you have no idea what "lugubrious" means (it means "gloomy," by the way), choice E shouldn't look too good. Resourceful festivities? What would that mean? So go with **C.**

Ex. **Taken aback when his friend's e-mail threatened to "hunt him down and take him out," Eliot's ----------- lasted for full seconds**

COMMEND: PRAISE

before he remembered that his generally ---------- friend had warned him that her e-mail account had recently been hacked.*

   a. astonishment / succinct
          d. consternation / docile

   b. bewilderment / admonishing
     e. malice / embittered

   c. apathy / intensified

So our words . . . again, the first blank is harder, so let's turn to the second. Eliot was worried his friend might have been trying to kill him, but it turns out the e-mail was from some other punk. (SAT questions would never be this risqué, by the way, even this minorly risqué.) The friend is generally not a murderer. So we could say "nice."

For the first blank, we need something that Eliot would feel if his friend threatened to kill him. How about "shock."

So the sentence is now:

Taken aback when his friend's e-mail threatened to "hunt him down and take him out," Eliot's <u>shock</u> lasted for full seconds before he remembered that his generally <u>nice</u> friend had warned him that her e-mail account had recently been hacked.

Match the second blank first. Which means "nice"?

a. succinct NAH

b. admonishing NAH

c. intensified NAH

d. docile SURE

e. embittered NAH

Now let's check the first blank of D to make sure it works. "Consternation"? Even if you don't know what it means, it sounds possible. **D** is right. See? Even if you don't know "malice" or "apathy," you can get the question right.

*True story!

What if you really have no idea what to do on a question?

Ex. **Ligurian Lions of Burnt Sea Foam are intrinsically calisthalacious, which means, of course, that they are both yodelastic and ----------.**

    a. avaricious   d. burgeoning

    b. cute   e. insane

    c. inquisitive

Stop trying to figure it out. This sentence is totally a joke.

RULE #3: *If You Have No Idea on a Question, and It Comes Early in a Section, Guess an Easy Word. If It Comes Late in a Section, Guess a Hard Word.*

Sometimes you'll get a sentence that just bowls you over, like in the (facetious) example above. If you have to guess, you can fall back on statistics. When you come across a group of sentence completion questions, (roughly) the last half is hard, and the first half is easy. So what we'd guess for this question would depend on where it appeared.

If the question appeared as number two out of seven, say, we'd guess "cute," "inquisitive," or "insane."

If it were fifth out of six, say, we'd guess "avaricious" or "burgeoning."

It's a really inexact science, but this strategy can come in handy if you're totally screwed. Much better to use Rules #1 or #2, as hard questions can sometimes have answers that are easy words. Rule #3 is just a fallback.

The correct answer, by the way, is obviously "cute." Unless it's "insane." Or "avaricious." As long as you don't put "inquisitive." Please. AS IF.

Critical Reading: How Insightful Thinking Will Foul You Up Every Time

After the sentence completion questions, you'll face reading comprehension passages. I know they're boring, and that's the rub: *Your greatest challenge will be your own lack of interest.* It's a psychological truth that your brain will only bother to comprehend that which interests it. We're constantly sorting information throughout our day, holding on to what's useful and discarding what's not, and that tendency doesn't shut off just because you're taking the SAT. If you go in thinking that the reading passages are boring, then guess what? You won't process the information in any meaningful way. Your options are two:

1. Take a genuine interest in the material. My students will scream their denials, but the reading passages are often pretty fascinating. They *haven't*, as some of the guidebooks will sound cool by telling you, been chosen for their dullness. There have recently been passages about Napster.com, the reasons young animals play, and snippets of best-selling fiction. I still remember the passage on my (1996) SAT, about how we humans evolved to find some environments more beautiful only because they're safer. So go in with a positive attitude, and you just might get excited by a passage. Or at least excited enough to get a high score.

2. Fake it. Here's where you theater stars will have an advantage. Slip a boa around your neck, dangle a cigarette holder from your fingertips, and prepare a monologue about how *simply marvelous* you find the reading passages. Recite this monologue before beginning to read the passage

CONFLAGRATION: FIRE

Hilariously Biased Questions of SATs Past and the Hilariously Politically Correct Passages They Inspired

The SAT has long been challenged over concerns of bias. While in a recent year the average SAT score of whites was 1060, the average hispanic student's score was 922, and the average black test taker's score was 857. The inequality isn't just about race: Males outscored females by about 40 points.

Which shouldn't fire up all of you neo-conservatives. Males might outscore females on the SAT, for example, but that points to a failure of the test, because females consistently earn higher college GPAs than males.

And what may appear to be lower performance based on race could actually be lower performance based on income level. Students from wealthier families outscore those from poorer families, and racial minorities are underrepresented in the higher income brackets.

Why do richer students do better? Of course better educational opportunities are a factor, but the class bias is also more insidious. Two famous examples (from back when the SAT had analogies) are the "DIVIDEND: STOCKHOLDER" and "OARSMAN: REGATTA" questions. Stocks and dividends are more commonly discussed in houses with money, of course, and a regatta (a series of boat races) is a WASPy event that involves cardigans knotted around necks. Not surprisingly, blacks underperformed on the regatta question, with only 22 percent of them getting it right, compared to 53 percent of whites. It's one thing to include hard vocabulary, it's quite another to include vocabulary that only students from certain cultural backgrounds have come across.

But that was years ago; the SAT is better now, right?

Well, no. Not entirely.

The Critical Reading section bends over backward to accommodate minorities, often to comic effect. You're guaranteed to come across a couple of passages about minorities on every test, virtually always about their succeeding against great odds. There are a preponderance of female scientists and astronauts in the sentence completion questions (you can use this to your advantage, actually: If you have a question about a minority, chances are the correct answer is going to have a positive spin).

But whatever cultural inclusion memo circulated to the Critical Reading writers failed to make it to the math department. One recent math question deals with the intricacies of calculating a cab fare based on a fixed charge plus a certain amount per mile. All my students take cabs. But are poor kids plunking down $20 a day to take a cab to school? No chance. Another asks students to calculate the time zone difference if one plane flies from New York to San Francisco and another returns the same day. If you've been fortunate enough to jet about the United States, or have a parent who flies on business, you've had to deal with the three-hour difference. If you live in Biloxi, and your parents own a dry cleaner, see how intuitive calculating the East Coast/West Coast time zone change is.

CONSENSUS: AGREEMENT

(avoiding the nervous glances of your neighbors). In all honesty, some (boa-less) version of this strategy helps my students all the time. Take a moment to look away from the test before you begin reading the passage, tell yourself that you're going to be *so* into it, and only then begin reading. You'll be surprised how much this raises your comprehension.

As far as how to read the passages, I officially recommend the approach that has you begin with the top left word and proceed, sweeping the page from left to right, down line by line until you reach the bottom right word. Read it, in other words.

Some old-fashioned strategy guides will have you skip reading the passage and only look back at the line numbers questions ask about. This tactic might have worked years ago, but increasingly, comprehension questions have required you to know things you won't be able to put together without at least skimming the entire passage.

If you find reading easy, simply read the passage and then begin doing the questions.

If you find that you frequently read a paragraph, only to find that you haven't actually processed a word, then you need *to underline key phrases in the passage.* It doesn't matter a whole lot what you underline; merely physically interacting with the passage will keep your attention focused and prevent you from wondering, say, where you're going for lunch after, or where you'll apply if you get an 1800, or why the kid in front of you coughs wetly every time he scratches his back.

If you find reading comprehension passages impossibly

Pay special attention to the following words, which appear with amazing frequency on reading comprehension questions:

Anthropology=the study of man
Undermine=to destroy (think "to put a mine under")
Underscore=to underline/emphasize (it's this thing: __, which at some point in prehistory was a key on typewriters used to underline words)
Underline=to emphasize

hard, underline key parts of a passage *and* write two or three words in the margin by each paragraph summarizing what it was about. A typical passage for you might look like this one:

The following night they transferred their game to <u>an Italian restaurant</u>. In the glow of candlelight and Bolognese she looked <u>even hotter</u>. She rested the backs of her arms on
Creepy Date! 5   the table's edge as he spoke, as if waiting for him to <u>inject her with morphine</u>. By the time he asked for the check she was clearly charmed and he was impressed <u>(if a bit bored) at his predictable dating prowess</u>.
10   From Aaron's side the busboy hauled a ravaged dish of olives, now only felty pits in oil, and a pool of beef juice from which a piece of garnish sprang like a fountain. <u>Darlene was "still working!"</u> on an
He's not into her… 15   appetizer salad plate which harbored a pair of cherry tomatoes and a mass of red onion. She absently stroked the gooseflesh and down of her arm as she tortured the onions
but he's a jerk anyway. with her fork. Aaron stared at her and
20   managed <u>to concoct an expression</u> that announced he <u>found her beauty dumbfounding</u>.

Source: Pretentious Short Story Written by Your Author in College

Even if you find it hard to get into the passage, scribbling all over it will force you to engage with it anyway.

Some passages are comparative; you'll be given two viewpoints on an issue and will have a long set of questions to answer. Your approach to these will be the same as it was on the other reading passages, with one exception: *Don't read both passages at first.* If you read both passages right away, you'll have forgotten what Passage 1 was about by the time you get to the questions. Just read the first passage, and answer the questions that pertain to it. Then read the second passage, and answer the questions that pertain to it. Now you're ready to answer the questions that require you to compare the passages. So:

1 Read Passage 1.
2 Answer the questions for Passage 1 (you can tell which questions by the line numbers they refer to, or they'll say "Passage 1" in the question).
3 Read Passage 2.
4 Answer the questions for Passage 2.
5 Answer the remaining questions.

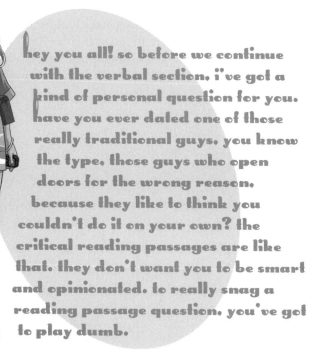

hey you all! so before we continue with the verbal section, i've got a kind of personal question for you. have you ever dated one of those really traditional guys, you know the type, those guys who open doors for the wrong reason, because they like to think you couldn't do it on your own? the critical reading passages are like that. they don't want you to be smart and opinionated. to really snag a reading passage question, you've got to play dumb.

Aiming Low: Plot Summary Is Your Dreamboat

Remember, the Critical Reading section used to be called Reading Comprehension, and that's *the only thing that's being tested—what you've comprehended.* Some students, particularly smarty-pants, pick the answer choice that sounds like something they're supposed to say in English class, something analytical, when the correct answer is always the one that sounds like dumb old *plot summary.*

Guarantee it, you're probably overestimating the test.

For practice, try the following excerpt:

> By the sixteenth century the English monarchy, recognizing the growing use of heraldic arms to represent and mark noble families, realized that a system must be in place to regulate their use. Henry VIII created the post of King of Arms, whose sole job was to visit the countryside and solicit evidence from the local gentry of their right to bear heraldic arms. These visitations threatened the very core of a country nobleman's honor, and were dreaded by the landed gentry. They were undoubtedly pleased to see that such visitations had all but ceased by the end of the seventeenth century.

The discussion of the regulation of heraldic arms suggests that English noblemen during Henry VIII's time

    (A)   allowed inspections of their arms only when promised other benefits by the crown.

    (B)   believed that their conviction in their right to bear heraldic arms should have been adequate proof.

    (C)   were tenacious enough to make sure their way of thinking eventually won out.

(D)   did not wish to have the crown
       question the validity of their
       heraldic arms.
(E)   were adept at political negotiation.

Now listen up, especially you brainiacs. Sure, there are some hardish words in there ("heraldic"), but if you read carefully, it's not too tricky to get what's going on here: Henry VIII didn't trust that the nobles weren't tricking him by falsifying their coats-of-arms, so he sent a guy out to check on them.

As you pick your answer, imagine yourself as someone with perfect reading skills but no intellectual ability. *The correct answer is the one that doesn't require any insight.*

In other words, be careful of answer choices that sound intelligent—because they're generally wrong. In reading comprehension the right answer is the one that is basically and simply true. Here, that's **D**. The nobles didn't want Henry messing in their business, end of story.

You might have been tempted to put A, that the nobles "*allowed inspections of their arms only when promised other benefits by the crown*" (they'd have made sure they profited from all their trouble, right?), or B, they "*believed that their conviction in their right to bear heraldic arms should have been adequate proof*" (if they didn't think arms needed to be inspected, they probably didn't want anything else to be looked to for proof, right?). Or C or E are probably true, because the political tides eventually turned in the nobles' favor. But think of it this way: for any of those to be right, D would have to be right, too! You can't have the nobles negotiating hard, or making further demands about whether they need proof, if they're not irked at Henry in the first place. And if D *has* to be true for the others to work, then D's our clear choice.

The right answer in reading comprehension is the one that's simply, basically true—not the one that sounds the smartest.

Let's try a typical short passage with two questions.

Ex.

Questions 1–2 are based on the following passage.

As early as 1769 that mighty Nimrod,
Daniel Boone, curious to hunt buffaloes, of
which he had heard weird reports, passed
through the Cumberland Gap and brought back
5 news of a wonderful country awaiting the plow.
A hint was sufficient. Singly, in pairs, and in
groups, settlers followed the trail he had blazed.
A great land corporation, the Transylvania
Company, emulating the merchant adventurers
10 of earlier times, secured a huge grant of territory
and sought profits in quit rents from lands sold to
farmers.

By the outbreak of the Revolution there
were several hundred people in the Kentucky
15 region. Like the older colonists, they did not
relish quit rents, and their opposition wrecked
the Transylvania Company. They even carried
their protests into the Continental Congress in
1776, for by that time they were our "embryo
fourteenth colony."

1. In the context of the passage, the nearest meaning of "Nimrod" (line 1) is someone who
   (A) is particularly suited to rugged terrain.
   (B) takes a particular interest in colonial history.
   (C) enjoys hunting.
   (D) was born in the modern-day Kentucky region.
   (E) is unable to live up to his own expectations.

2. The author places quotation marks around "embryo fourteenth colony" (line 19) to emphasize
   (A) the transience of a phrase.
   (B) the broad scientific education of the Congress's members.
   (C) the congressmen's reluctance to add another colony and diminish their own individual power.
   (D) the growing importance of a region.
   (E) the futility of the Congress's efforts to reinstate the Transylvania Company.

After reading the passage (and marking it up, if necessary), we turn to the questions.

The first refers us to the Nimrod line, right at the beginning. Let's see what clues we can pick up around it:

It applies to Daniel Boone.

He was "curious to hunt."

He discovered that Kentucky is a good farming area.

That's all the passage directly tells us about this "Nimrod." Choice A sounds *likely* (he was a settler, so he'd be well adapted to rugged terrain), and B, D, and E sound like interesting arguments a history student would make, statements that, if backed up with evidence, would make a teacher very happy. *But reading comprehension doesn't go for "likely."* We want the answer that is stated in the passage. Since Boone was "curious to hunt," only **C** makes sense, that a Nimrod "enjoys hunting."

For the next question:

Choice A sounds wicked smart. "Transience of a phrase," indeed! But it doesn't have a meaning here. (Transience, by the way, is a synonym for impermanence, which means not staying around for long.)

Choice B, likewise, is attractive because it seems like a good thing to know. But it's not stated in the passage. Likewise with C and E.

Only **D** captures what the passage is saying, which is that Kentucky was becoming an important region for the colonies.

Avoiding Strong Wording (Because No One Falls in Love with a Desperate Answer Choice)

The best way to approach a reading comprehension question is by process of elimination—rather than searching for the right answer, try to find the four wrong ones. You'll be picking out any flaws you can, and finding any excuse to nail 'em like a zit. The only answer that survives your assault will be the one that has nothing wrong with it. And how does an answer choice survive? In short, it has to be meek, boring, and unobtrusive.

Which brings us to our next Critical Reading comprehension rule: *Avoid answer choices with strong wording.* Anything that states an interesting claim or has a point of view is a target. While sophisticated sentiments would make great theses for an essay, they're taboo on reading comprehension (which is why I say the SAT sends mixed

DECOROUS: WELL-BEHAVED

messages—it encourages a point of view on the essay, and then penalizes you for it on reading comprehension).

Here are words to avoid in your answer choices:

ALWAYS	UNDOUBTEDLY
NEVER	FULLY
MUST	COULD ONLY
EXTREMELY	

On the other side of the coin, these wishy-washy words often come along with right answers:

MIGHT BE	MINORLY
MAY BE	COULD BE SEEN AS
COULD BE	ARGUABLY
SUGGESTS/IMPLIES	

Try the following example, in which the question has been translated into Russian. (Don't worry; none of your reading passages will be in Russian. Probably.)

Ваш книжный автор высоко впечатлен вашим знанием русского языка (линия 14). Готовый отвечать

    a.   downplays the impact Orthodox religion had on young Russian women's lives.

    b.   could be interpreted as suggesting that the Russians were innately adaptable.

    c.   is against the current academic interest in Russian history.

    d.   promotes, without reservation, the inclusion of women in St. Petersburg college life.

e.   sees modern Russian women
as fully in control of their lives.

Okay—put on your wishy-washy meter. Which seems the most vague? That's right, "could be interpreted as suggesting." **B** would most likely be the right answer on this question.

Of course, you don't want to apply this rule exclusively. There will always be exceptions. But if you're debating between two answer choices that seem equally valid (and it'll happen frequently), go with the one that's got the more ambiguous phrasing. My reasoning is simple: Basically *anything* "could be interpreted as suggesting" something. I can truthfully say that some speech of the Pope's *could be* interpreted as suggesting that miniskirts should come back in style. It's not likely. But sure, his speech *could be interpreted* that way—it's in the realm of possibility. That just can't be wrong.

Where to Look for Answers, or Why Comprehending the Whole Passage Is So OoF (Out of Fashion)

Here's a bone the reading comprehension passages throw to you: You rarely need to keep the whole passage in your head. That's probably your greatest fear going in, that you'll have to figure out how the fourth paragraph reflects on the second, and what the overall message is. Nah. You're only responsible for small snippets of text. As long as you get the overall gist of the passage, you don't need to put any more thought into the larger issues.

To help you zoom in properly, follow two simple rules. The first one is this:

If you're given a line number, you're responsible for the material one thumb's width above and one thumb's width below the line number.

(If you don't trust your thumb size, go for about five lines above/
below.)

      Poop poop poop poop poop. Poop poop
      poop poop? Poop poop poop poop poop
      poop poop poop poop poop poop poop poop
      poop poop poop poop poop poop poop poop
5   poop poop poop poop poop poop poop poop
      poop poop poop poop poop poop.
        Poop poop poop poop poop poop
      poop poop poop poop poop poop poop poop
      poop; poop poop poop poop poop poop
10 poop poop poop poop poop poop poop poop
      poop poop poop poop poop poop poop poop
      poop poop poop poop poop poop: Poop
      poop poop poop poop poop poop. Poop
      poop poop poop poop poop (poop poop
15 poop) poop poop poop poop poop poop
      poop poop poop poop.
        Poop poop poop poop poop poop
      poop poop poop poop poop poop poop poop
      poop poop poop poop poop poop poop poop
20 poop poop poop poop—poop poop poop
      poop poop poop poop poop poop poop poop
      poop poop.

**In lines 11–12, what does the author suggest by her use of the phrase
"poop poop"?**

We know that the answer will have to be found within a thumb's width
above and a thumb's width below the line numbers given, or from about
line 7 through line 16.

      Poop poop poop poop poop. Poop poop
      poop poop? Poop poop poop poop poop
      poop poop poop poop poop poop poop poop
      poop poop poop poop poop poop poop poop

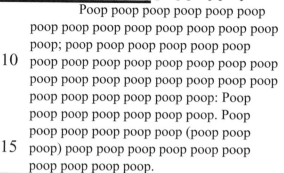

5   poop poop poop poop poop poop poop poop
poop poop poop poop poop poop poop.

Poop poop poop poop poop poop
poop poop poop poop poop poop poop poop
poop; poop poop poop poop poop poop

10 poop poop poop poop poop poop poop poop
poop poop poop poop poop poop poop poop
poop poop poop poop poop poop: Poop
poop poop poop poop poop poop. Poop
poop poop poop poop poop (poop poop

15 poop) poop poop poop poop poop poop
poop poop poop poop.

Poop poop poop poop poop poop
poop poop poop poop poop poop poop poop
poop poop poop poop poop poop poop poop

20 poop poop poop poop—poop poop poop
poop poop poop poop poop poop poop poop
poop poop.

Responsible for this material

This rule has three very important implications: *First* is that—who knew?—poop is a subject worthy of academic study. *Second* is that you can always just zero in on the immediate area to find your answer (keeping in mind, as we covered in the last section, that the correct answer will be the one that best *summarizes*—not analyzes—the passage). *Third* is that, when you're given a line number, you mustn't read just that line—*the immediate context is as important as the line itself.*

What if a question doesn't give you a line number? More often than not, it will be a "primary purpose" question, which is one that asks you something like:

Ex. **The author's main intention in writing about poop is to show that poop**

a. **poop poop poop!**

b. **poop poop poop.**

c. **poop (poop) poop.**

d. **poop; poop; poop.**

e. **poops.**

Where to look for such an answer? We weren't given a line number!

SAT passages are generally taken from real, published sources, then edited so that their thesis (main point) is summarized in the first bit and the last bit. So if you aren't given a line number, your answer can be found in the first thumb length and last thumb length of the passage.

Poop poop poop poop poop. Poop poop poop poop? Poop poop poop poop poop poop poop poop poop poop poop poop poop poop poop poop poop poop poop poop

Responsible for this section

5 poop poop poop poop poop poop poop poop poop poop poop poop poop poop poop.

      Poop poop poop poop poop poop poop poop poop poop poop poop poop poop poop; poop poop poop poop poop poop

10 poop poop poop poop poop poop poop poop poop poop poop poop poop poop poop poop poop poop poop poop poop poop: Poop poop poop poop poop poop poop. Poop poop poop poop poop poop (poop poop

15 poop) poop poop poop poop poop poop poop poop poop poop.

      Poop poop poop poop poop poop poop poop poop poop poop poop poop poop poop poop poop poop poop poop poop poop poop poop poop poop—poop poop poop poop poop poop poop poop poop poop poop poop.

Responsible for this section

To summarize: If you get a line number, look a little bit above and below for your answer; if you aren't given a line number, look at the first and last bits.

Before we move on, there's one more problem type you'll come across, the "word in context" question. It might ask you, for example, what the word "poop" means in the context of line 15. What you don't want to do is just go with the answer that seems closest to your personal definition of poop. All five definitions the question offers are legitimate. Instead, you have to judge based on context. So treat it like a sentence completion. Pretend the quoted word was a blank. What would your word be for that blank? Then match that to the answer choices.

Ex. ... **The foreman knew no one was at the front door to greet the guests, so he dispatched his sister to go do what she could to make them comfortable ...**

In context, the word "dispatched" (line 2) most nearly means
a. hastened   d. killed
b. sent off   e. mailed
c. launched

Cross out "dispatched." What would you put instead? "Sent"? Or maybe "asked"? What's closest to those words? **B**, "sent off."

  Now we'll try a reading passage that's neither in Russian nor about poop.

Practice Reading Comprehension Passage

Remember, get yourself psyched up, even if you have to fake it!

  Oh boy, reading comp!!!!!!

Questions 1–6 are based on the following passage.

The third person in the great Florentine trinity of painters was Leonardo da Vinci (1452–1519), the other two being Michelangelo and Raphael. He greatly influenced the school of Milan,
5   and has usually been classed with the Milanese, yet he was educated in Florence, in the workshop of Verrocchio, and was so universal in thought and methods that he hardly belongs to any school.

He has been named a realist, an idealist,
10   a magician, a wizard, a dreamer, and finally a scientist, by different writers, yet he was none of these things while being all of them—a fully rounded, universal man, learned in many

15   departments and excelling in whatever he undertook. He had a scientific and experimental way of looking at things. That is perhaps to be regretted, since it resulted in his experimenting with everything and completing little of anything. His different tastes and pursuits pulled him
20   different ways, and his knowledge made him skeptical of his own powers. He pondered and thought how to reach up higher, how to penetrate deeper, how to realize more comprehensively, and in the end he gave up in despair. He could
25   not fulfill his ideal of the head of Christ or the head of Mona Lisa, and after years of labor he

Occurred on the Job, Park Avenue at 87th Street:
The hard part about looking eighteen: tutor forbidden from going upstairs by doorman, who won't listen when tutor explains that he isn't actually an illicit boyfriend.

left them unfinished. The problem of human life, the spirit, the world engrossed him, and all his creations seem impregnated with the

30 psychological, the mystical, the unattainable, the hidden.

He was no religionist, though he painted the religious subject with feeling; he was not in any sense a classicist, nor had he any care for the

35 antique marbles, which he considered a study of nature at second-hand. He was more in love with physical life without being an enthusiast over it. His regard for contours, rhythm of line, blend of light with shade, study of atmosphere,

40 perspective, trees, animals, and humanity show that though he examined nature scientifically, he pictured it aesthetically. In his types there is much sweetness of soul, charm of disposition, dignity of mien, even grandeur and majesty of presence.

45 His people we would like to know better. They are full of life, intelligence, sympathy; they have fascination of manner, winsomeness of mood, grace of bearing. We see this in his best-known work—the *Mona Lisa* of the Louvre. It has much

50 allurement of personal presence, with a depth and abundance of soul altogether charming.

Technically, Leonardo was not a handler of the brush superior in any way to his Florentine contemporaries. He knew all the methods and

55 mediums of the time, and did much to establish oil-painting among the Florentines, but he was never a painter like Titian, or even Correggio or Andrea del Sarto. A splendid draughtsman, a man of invention, imagination, grace, elegance,

60 and power, he nevertheless carried more by mental penetration and aesthetic sense than by his technical skill. He was one of the great men of the Renaissance, and deservedly holds a place in the front rank.

65 Though Leonardo's accomplishment seems slight because of the little that is left to us, he had a great following not only among the Florentines but at Milan, where Vincenzo Foppa

70 had started a school in the Early Renaissance time. Leonardo was there for fourteen years, and his artistic personality influenced many painters to adopt his type and methods. Bernardino Luini (1475–1532) was the most prominent of the

75 disciples. He cultivated Leonardo's sentiment, style, subjects, and composition in his middle period, but later on developed independence and originality. He came at a period of art when that earnestness of characterization which marked the early men was giving way to gracefulness of

80 recitation, and that was the chief feature of his art.

1. The author's primary purpose in this passage is to
   (A)   identify the main elements and impact of da Vinci's art.
   (B)   analyze artistic trends of the sixteenth century.
   (C)   compare da Vinci's works to those of Michelangelo and Raphael.
   (D)   evaluate the extent to which religious material contributed to da Vinci's work.
   (E)   analyze competing claims about da Vinci's legacy.

2. That "he hardly belongs to any school" (line 8) most nearly means that da Vinci
   (A)   was undereducated.
   (B)   had interests diverse enough to render them difficult to classify.
   (C)   can't be effectively compared to either Michelangelo or Raphael.
   (D)   can never be identified with any one trend in art.
   (E)   avoided political movements of his era.

3. In context, "universal" (line 13) most nearly means
   (A) eternal
   (B) widespread
   (C) unavoidable
   (D) well-rounded
   (E) unanimous

4. What about da Vinci's work does the author identify as being "charming" (line 51)?
   (A) his technical skill
   (B) his modesty about his own masterwork, the *Mona Lisa*
   (C) his interest in the hard sciences
   (D) the absolute inconsequence of his work
   (E) the depth of his characterizations

5. In the fourth paragraph (lines 52–64) the author suggests which of the following about da Vinci's legacy?
   (A) He was inferior to many painters of his day.

(B) He would have done better to have studied painting at a Florentine school.
(C) Critics are too unabashed in their praise of him.
(D) He was a master despite, not because of, his technique.
(E) He was famous largely because of the swiftness of his artistic process.

6. The author introduces the example of Bernardino Luini (line 72) primarily in order to
   (A) demonstrate how da Vinci's shortcomings were eventually overcome by his followers.
   (B) identify the impact of da Vinci's art on the next generation.
   (C) point to an artistic trend that would last for centuries.
   (D) show the absolute similarities between da Vinci's art and that of a follower.
   (E) emphasize a generally accepted theory about da Vinci's art.

Source: The Project Gutenberg EBook of *a Text-Book of the History of Painting*, by John C. Van Dyke

Answers:

1. A
2. B
3. D
4. E
5. D
6. B

Explanations:

A *primary purpose* question requires us to look at the first thumb-width and the last thumb-width of the passage, where we find that da Vinci was a great Florentine painter, and that eventually some

DISINGENUOUS: FAKE

"earnestness of characterization" gives way to some "gracefulness of recitation." Whatever those are.

B doesn't match, because it's too broad.

C doesn't work, because Michelangelo and Raphael don't come up again after the first bit.

D doesn't work, because religion doesn't come in the first and last thumb-widths at all.

E sounds smart, but we don't see any "competing claims" stated. It's too much analysis instead of *plot summary*.

A therefore has to be our answer.

2 We're pointed to line 8, so let's re-read 3–13.

A, C, and E don't work because they discuss issues or ideas that aren't brought up in the passage.

D doesn't work, because it's *too strongly worded*. Sure, he's hard to pin down, but da Vinci can *never* be identified with any one movement? That's going too far.

B is our answer.

3 We should treat a *word in context* question like a sentence completion. What word or phrase would you put instead of "universal"?

"Broad"? "Multidimensional"?

Now let's look at our choices. The closest to "broad" would be **D**, "well-rounded." Let's read it in the sentence—if our answer choice is correct, it should sound perfect. "—a fully rounded, **well-rounded** man, learned in many departments and excelling in whatever he undertook." Sounds good to me!

4 Another line number—let's look at lines 44–54.

A doesn't work because the author's actually down on da Vinci's technical skill (lines 52–53).

B isn't *plot summary*—we find no mention of any modesty on da Vinci's part.

Multidimensional! Ooh, good word! Just don't call me a "broad."

Don't Keep Doing the Example Problems

You've got your test book in front of you, you're hella nervous, and the proctor has just asked you to begin. Whoosh!

First problem you're going to see on each Critical Reading and Writing section is an example, and it's always the same.

These will *always* be your examples. Read them now. Get over them. Please. You'll be eager, you'll be ready to pounce on the first question-like thing you come across, but don't waste time doing the example every time.

Example:

Hoping to ------- the dispute, negotiators proposed a compromise that they felt would be ------- to both labor and management.

   a. enforce/useful
   b. end/divisive
   c. overcome/unattractive
   d. extend/satisfactory
   e. resolve/acceptable   **(E)**

Example:

Laura Ingalls Wilder published her first book <u>and she was sixty-five years old then</u>.

   a. and she was sixty-five years old then
   b. when she was sixty-five
   c. at age sixty-five years old
   d. upon the reaching of sixty-five years
   e. at the time when she was sixty-five   **(B)**

Example:

<u>The other</u> delegates and <u>him</u> <u>immediately</u> accepted the resolution <u>drafted by</u>
   A   B   C   D

the neutral states. <u>No Error</u>
          E   **(B)**

DISINTERESTED: UNBIASED

C refers to the fact that da Vinci was a scientist. But that was much earlier in the passage (a bad sign, since we should only really be looking at the immediate ten lines), and refutes what the author states to be da Vinci's charm.

D is too strong. "Absolute inconsequence"? No way; why would there be a reading passage about him, then?

E has to be our answer.

5 We have a whole paragraph to fixate on this time.

A is *too strong*. Da Vinci may not have had the technical skill of the named painters, but he's still "one of the great men of the Renaissance."

B isn't *plot summary* enough. Maybe it's true, but it's not in the passage. Likewise for C and E.

D is our answer.

6 Now we're looking from line 68 to the end. We see that Luini came after da Vinci, and modeled him for a while, then went on to do his own (good) things.

A is being too critical of da Vinci. It's evident by now that the author's a big fan of da Vinci—he's not identifying any "shortcomings" here.

C goes too far—*plot summary* of the passage doesn't reveal the author saying that anything will last for centuries (even if you've studied painting and know about da Vinci's long-term impact, it's not in the passage, so you can't choose it).

D is *too strong*. "Absolute"? Nah. There are similarities, but they aren't incredible similarities. Luini diverges from da Vinci toward the end of his life.

E supposes there's a generally accepted theory out there about da Vinci's art. Maybe there is, but it's not *plot summary*.

B is our answer.

DISSEMINATE: SPREAD

PART III

MATH

(Even Cheaper Tricks
from Your Tutor,
with Commentary
from Various Sassy
Students)

Relax: You Learned All the Math You Needed to Know by the Eighth Grade

If you'll permit me a page of boring logistics:

You will have three Math sections on your SAT, each one slightly different from the next.

One will be a twenty-five-minute "standard" Math section, containing twenty problems, each accompanied by five answer choices.

One will be a twenty-five-minute section that starts with eight standard five-choice questions, followed by ten "grid-in" questions. These don't have answer choices, and require you instead to bubble in the numbers that correspond to your answer.

The last section will run only twenty minutes, and will contain sixteen standard, five-choice questions.

Each run of questions will go from easy to hard, with all questions worth the same amount. That's kind on the part of the test makers, since you'll naturally start with the easiest questions; if you leave questions at the end blank, they're questions you were less likely to get right anyway. Another way the SAT is surprisingly un-evil.

Once you learn that Math sections go from easy to hard, you might assume that the questions will start with counting dimes and culminate in calculating the orbits of star systems. It may come as a shock,

If you're a top-scoring SAT-er, grid-ins will be your main battleground in math. Because you won't have any answer choices, it will be much harder to catch *careless errors*. Work through all of your grid-in questions twice, preferably using different methods each time.

therefore, when you find out that none of the fancy math you're currently studying will do you a lick of good on the SAT. That's right: Everyone who does well on the math, even those weenies getting 800s each time, is using concepts that she learned back in the eighth grade. Nothing much more complex than πr^2. Baby stuff.

Why, then, does anyone miss anything?

Because the questions are damn hard. And they're hard because they require advanced reasoning, not advanced knowledge.

The thinking behind avoiding advanced math is a good one: The SAT shouldn't test any concepts that poorer school systems may be unequipped to teach, as that's unfair to the bright kid who happens to go to a crummy high school. SAT math therefore focuses on reasoning instead of achievement, which essentially means perverting otherwise respectable math concepts into grotesque beasts.

For example:

SCHOOL **(straightforward):**	Please add 4.15 and $4x^2$, if $x = 1.3$
SAT **(perverted):**	What's the sum of all the numbers from −34 through 40?
	(Yeah, there's a formula for that. See page 154.)
SCHOOL **(straightforward):**	What is the definition of an integer?
SAT **(perverted):**	What is the least non-negative even integer?
	(Erp? See page 151.)
SCHOOL **(straightforward):**	If you drive 400 miles in 8 hours, what is your rate of speed?
SAT **(perverted):**	If you drive to school at 30 mph and return at 40 mph, what is your average speed?
	(And it's not 35 mph, wise-ass. See page 93.)
SCHOOL **(straightforward):**	What is the perimeter of a right triangle with legs of length 3 and 4?

SAT (perverted): If a triangle has integer sides, two of which are 3 and 4, what is the maximum value of its perimeter?
(Crying? See page 141.)

The nice thing, of course, is that you needn't feel nervous if you've skipped math class for the last few years. The SAT is decidedly retro. Just bone up on the concepts I'm about to lay out here, and put all of that recently learned, more overwrought math to one side. You hear me? No more tan, sin, and cos, which sounded like a death metal band, anyway.

We're about to time-travel to eighth grade, so go get your Clay Aiken T-shirt and braces on and meet me outside of sex ed.

A math teacher sensually whispers the answers to the problems on the last page:

10.91
225
"a positive or negative number without a fractional part, i.e. {-2, -1, 0, 1, 2}"
0
50 mph
34.29 mph
12
13

Avoiding Careless Errors:
Three Essential Keys to Math Success

Key #1. Mark Your Booklet Up

If your test booklet is pristine, you're in trouble: You're either being too cocky and doing problems in your head, or you've gone into the test unprepared and are tear-staining the pages. Either way, you've screwed up.

Back when I was preparing for the SAT, in between listening to Paula Abdul and learning about this new-fangled "Internet," I decided to *circle the numbers* of any problems that I skipped and wanted to go back to, and put a * next to ones that I had answered but felt unsure about. Then, once I'd made it through the whole section, I first went back to the circled problems, and then spent the rest of the time looking back over the *'d ones. (This approach, by the way, works equally well for the Critical Reading and Writing sections.) Feel free to alter the symbols, if *s seem too 1996. But don't draw ☺s, because they take too much time.

If after you score a practice test you find that you've made more than two careless errors in a Math section, start *underlining key words in the questions.* Anything factual needs to be marked, especially words like "positive", "integer", "except", "greater than"—anything that fundamentally alters what the question is asking. This will force you to read more actively and not overlook key elements of a question.

Make sure you mark the problems you want to go back to only in your test booklet, not on your answer sheet. Otherwise the grading machine might get confused. And confused grading machine = not getting into college = living in your parents' attic.

Key #2. Use All Your Time

It's one thing to finish a Verbal or Writing section early and take a nap with the time you have left over—those sections are more conceptual, and you're less likely to have made an outright error. But on Math . . . don't you dare take a break once you've finished. For SAT math is the Lair of Careless Errors, where even those who have won Westinghouse Science Fellowships regularly miss problems just by overlooking a middling detail. Look, no one's expecting you to take your practice tests like an obsessive madman, but on the real thing, *you'd better work up until the very end.*

When you're reworking problems to check your work, best is to try to solve a problem a totally different way. It's amazing how, when you rework a problem using the same method, you can make the same error all over again. Using a different method of solving can get you around it.

Ex. **If $3^{3x} = 9^{x+4}$, what is the value of x?**

   a. 5   d. 8
   b. 6   e. 9
   c. 7

There are at least two equally valid ways to solve this problem. The first involves reducing the 9 to 3^2, so that the bases are the same, like this:

$$3^{3x} = 3^{(2)(x+4)}$$

Then setting the exponents equal to each other:

$$3x = 2(x+4)$$
$$3x = 2x + 8 \quad \text{(Then subtract } 2x \text{ from both sides.)}$$
$$x = 8, \text{ Choice } \mathbf{D}$$

EBULLIENCE/EFFERVESCENCE: BUBBLINESS

Once you finish the section and use your remaining time to check over your work, you'll want to try doing it a different way.

The simpler (if less elegant) way to solve is by trial and error.

If $3^{3x} = 9^{x+4}$, what is the value of x?

Just try your answer choices, starting with A:

A: $3^{3x} = 9^{x+4}$

$3^{3(5)} = 9^{5+4}$

$3^{15} = 9^9$ (Now punch it into your calculator.)

$14,348,907 = 387,420,489?$

Nope!

Until you get to D:

D: $3^{3x} = 9^{x+4}$

$3^{3(8)} = 9^{8+4}$

$3^{24} = 9^{12}$

(calculating . . .)

$2.8 \times 10^{11} = 2.8 \times 10^{11}$

Yep!

If you can get the same answer to a problem two different ways, then you can be pretty sure it's right. And being sure will feel good once you're all done with the SAT and watching TV back home, or getting a piercing, or lying flat in the parking lot and drinking a Big Gulp, or what have you.

ELOQUENT: WELL-SPOKEN

Key# 3. Read the Question Over One Last Time Before You Bubble In Your Answer

One sneaky thing about SAT math problems is that they so often ask for odd things. It's like that lame riddle from third grade (which I thought was just hilarious at the time; I didn't have very many friends in the third grade):

At 7 A.M., a school bus has 20 students on board. At the first stop, the bus picks up 3 students and lets off 5. Then it picks up 4 students and lets off 10. At the next stop it picks up 6 and lets none off. Then it picks up 1 student, while 3 get off. Finally, it picks up 4 more students.

(Ready for the question?)

How many stops did the bus make?

Ha ha!

Okay, granted, this problem isn't nearly as mischievous in print, since you can just read back over it. And we have to ask ourselves—why on Earth was this school bus letting students *off* in the morning?

If a problem asks you to solve for an expression rather than a variable, it's generally because the expression is easier to solve for. The SAT's not just being cruel.

Ex. If $x^2 - y^2 = 60$, and $x - y = 15$, what does $x + y$ equal?
Solving for x and y individually will be tough, so don't do it. Solve for $x + y$ instead.

$x^2 - y^2 = 60$
$(x + y)(x - y) = 60$
(Since we're told that $x - y = 15$, let's substitute.)
$(x + y)15 = 60$
$x + y = 4$

Done! And a good three minutes earlier than if we solved for x and y separately.

ELUCIDATE: CLARIFY

What I want you to bring out of this, though, is that SAT math questions can frequently ask you for something unpredictable.

Ex. If $4(x^2 - 12x + 17) = 24$, $x - 11$ could equal which of the following?

    a. −4   d. 11

    b. 0   e. 17

    c. 4

You could easily do all the work to solve the problem, then bubble the answer in for what x is (D), and not what $x - 11$ is (the correct answer, **B**).

Hard math problems can take a while. By the time you've solved one, you'll have forgotten precisely what the question was asking. And since tests you've taken in school have almost always asked for a variable (x), rather than an expression ($x - 11$), you naturally assume that you were solving for x all along. *Re-reading the question before you bubble in your answer* can protect you from this common error.

Got Timing Issues?

If you find that you're leaving the last three (or more) questions blank at the end of a section, you're going to have to change your game plan.

CRITICAL READING: Skip the two last, hard sentence completions (the question type that begins the section). You'll buy yourself more time to do the reading passages, and prevent wasting time on questions that you could easily get wrong anyway.

MATH: The same goes for one math section in which you have eight multiple choice questions followed by ten grid-ins. If you're not able to finish these questions in time, skip the last two multiple choice questions—you can always go back to them at the end of the section if you have time.

In general, if you know you're going to have problems finishing the section, be choosy about which problems you do—if you glance at a problem and immediately know that it's going to take you a while, circle it and skip it.

EMINENT/PROMINENT: WELL-KNOWN

What to Do if You're Screwed

There's this odd macho vibe among math geeks, who often figure that the most advanced approach to a problem is the right one. And it is, if you're gunning for publication in a math journal, or if there's a teacher looking over your work who will whistle in amazement, or if you're trying to impress a geek goddess.

But no living person will ever see the answers you put on your SAT, much less the scratch work that led you to them. Your test book will be incinerated, and your bubble sheet will be graded by machines that couldn't care less how you came to your answer. This fact has a couple of implications:

1. It might impress your friends if you can divide 840 by 15 in your head (provided you have those kinds of friends, of course), but please please please *use your calculator to do computations on the SAT*. Mental calculations are a huge source of careless errors.

2. *Don't do a problem the official, textbook way if you can do it much more quickly through a cheap trick.*

And what are these cheap tricks? Before you throw in the towel on any math problem, you have to ask yourself whether you've applied the following two strategies.

The first of these two strategies . . .

That is, what you're about to read . . .

The very text that follows . . .

. . . is the most important rule in this book.

Take a deep breath.

EMPIRIC: FROM EXPERIENCE

#1. The Cheapest Trick of Them All: Plugging in Numbers

This approach takes complex algebra and reduces it to rote arithmetic, and it will slash even the most imposing problems to quivering puddles of easily solved goo. Honestly, effectively using this strategy can take down some real baddies, and it works on roughly 40 percent of the problems you'll face.

Basically, we're going to take a variable (like x) and swap it for a real number (like 2). You know you'll be able to plug in numbers on a problem if you have variables in your answer choices.

Ex. **Gwen Stefani can produce an album in a months. If Fergie takes four times as many months to produce an album, how many months will it take Fergie to produce seventeen albums, in terms of a?**

    A. $a/108$ D. $17a$

    B. $a/17$ E. $108a$

    C. a

Not an impossible problem to solve algebraically, but since we *can* solve it by plugging in numbers, we *should*. And how do we know we can plug in numbers? *Because there are variables (letters) in the answer choices,* that's why.

For the Math Purists Out There

Plugging in numbers works because it takes a process that describes an abstract totality (algebra), and applies it to one specific case. That is, if an algebraic expression is true for all values of x, it has to be true for any one value. We're just proving that a theoretical truism works in any individual case. There. Now does it sound like real math instead of a cheap trick?

So, back to the Gwen Stefani problem.

1 Let's say it takes Gwen 5 months to produce an album. That means we're letting $a = 5$.

2 Now the problem reads as follows:

Gwen Stefani can produce an album in 5 months. If Fergie takes four times as many months to produce an album, how many months will it take Fergie to produce seventeen albums, ~~in terms of a?~~

That means Fergie takes 4×5 months to produce an album, or 20 months. For seventeen albums, that means 17×20, or 340 months.

"Fergie produce 17 albums?! heaven forbid!"

3 Put a check next to 340, because it answers the question the problem posed ("how many months will it take Fergie to produce seventeen albums?").

4 Let's see which of our answer choices equals **340**, given that in step one we decided that $a = 5$.

A. 5/108? No.
B. 5/17? Nah.
C. 5? No way.
D. $17 \times 5 = 85$? Nope.
E. $108 \times 5 = 340$. Gotcha!

Let's try a different example.

"In terms of" is a useless phrase; cross it out whenever you see it; it just confuses things.

Plugging in Numbers:

1. Assign a value to the variable.
2. Work through the problem using that value.
3. Put a check mark next to the answer you get.
4. Plug the value from step one into the answer choices; whichever one matches the answer with the check mark is correct.

Ex. **If the price of a roll of Recycled Wood Chip Toilet Paper is reduced** 40% **and then raised** 40%**, the final price is what percent of the original price?**

A. 40%   D. 105%

B. 84%   E. 140%

C. 100%

Here we don't know for sure that we can plug in numbers, because there aren't any variables in the answer choices. *But we're going to turn to plugging in numbers because we can't think of any other way to solve this problem.* Plugging in numbers is our "I'm screwed" approach, our atom bomb, our pregnancy test.

100 is a great number to choose for percent problems. Makes the math so much easier.

1 Let's make our toilet paper $100.

2 40% of 100 is $40, so the new price is (100 − 40), or $60.

3 Now, we have to find 40% of 60. 40/100 × 60 = 24. So the toilet paper now costs $60 + $24, or $84.

4 84 is what percent of 100? Well, it's 84% of 100, duh.

5 The answer is **B**.

the answer isn't 100%? that's so weird. (pricey toilet paper, by the way. hope it's at least two-ply.)

Because this strategy is so important, let's try another example.

Ex. If $(xy)^{3/4} = m$, and $(xy)^{1/2} = n$, what is the value of $m \div n$, in terms of x and y?

A. $(xy)^{-2}$ D. x/y

B. $(xy)^{-5/4}$ E. $-3/8(xy)$

C. xy

Rough. We'll talk later about how to deal with fractional exponents (see page 119), but for now let's pretend (or not pretend) that we have no idea what to do. And by now we know that if we're screwed, it's time to plug in numbers!

1. Let x and y equal whatever you want. I'm going with $x = 3$ and $y = 4$.
$(3 \times 4)^{3/4}$, our calculator tells us, is 0.1551. So $m = 0.1551$.
Similarly, $n = (3 \times 4)^{1/2}$, or 3.4641.

2. What's $m \div n$? Well, Mr. Calculator says $0.1551 \div 3.4641 = 0.0448$.
Put a check mark next to 0.0448!

3. Which answer choice gives us 0.0448? Let's see.

A. $(xy)^{-2}$
$(12)^{-2}$ equals 0.0069. No.

B. $(xy)^{-5/4}$
$(12)^{-5/4}$ equals 0.0448. Woo-hoo!

C. xy
12. No.

D. x/y
3/4. Uh-uh.

E. $-3/8(xy)$
$-3/8(12)$ equals -4.5? No way.

Final Note on Plugging in Numbers:

It's very important that you try all the answer choices. If you pick a freak number, more than one choice may match your check-marked answer. If that happens, just assign a new value and try again.

See how great this is? Some really difficult problems become simple calculator jockeying. We'll come across some other good plugging-in-numbers candidates as we tackle more math. I'll point them out as they come.

   Such a cheap trick. But there's a lot riding on this test, so don't be above it. Using this strategy effectively can massively boost your score.

#2. The Second-Cheapest Trick of Them All: Trying the Answer Choices

This one might seem more intuitive to you. If you can't solve a problem by going forward, try going backward. It's a good way to check your work, and it's also a way to crack problems that are too hard to solve any other way.

Ex. At the annual televangelist convention, the caterers are instructed to bake one cinnamon loaf for every two guests, one chocolate loaf for every four guests, and one squid loaf for every six guests. **If the caterers baked 66 items total, how many guests attended the convention?**

A. 36   D. 72

B. 48   E. 80

C. 66

This one is pretty hard if you're trying to work forward. So let's turn to our "if you're screwed" strategies. Since it's not clear how we'd *plug in numbers*, let's *try answer choices*.

The best choice to start with is C, since if the middle value doesn't work, we can then decide whether we should go higher or lower.

So let's say there were 66 televangelists at the conference. In that case we'd need:

66/2, or 33 cinnamon loaves

66/4, or 16.5 chocolate loaves (Red flag: Are we really supposed to be getting halves of loaves?)

66/6, or 11 squid loaves

That makes 60.5 items total. Since it's supposed to be 66, we've just determined that answer choice C is incorrect. Let's go higher.

Choice D says there are 72 televangelists at the conference. Would that mean that 66 items were made? Let's see.

72/2, or 36 cinnamon loaves

72/4, or 18 chocolate loaves

72/6, or 12 squid loaves

That makes . . . 66 items total! Sweet. **D** is our best answer. I'll take the chocolate loaves; the squid loaves are all yours.

EQUIVOCATE: MISLEAD

Ex. **Two tribes are exchanging red-headed wives. Initially, the number of wives that the Yellow Tribe has is one-third the number that the Green Tribe has. If, after the Green Tribe gives the Yellow Tribe 15 wives, the number of wives in each tribe is equal, how many wives did the Yellow Tribe have initially?**

A. 15   D. 30

B. 20   E. 35

C. 25

SAT problems are generally far less perverse. Sadly.

This one doesn't give up its meaning easily, so go ahead and read it a couple of times and then report back.

Let's say we're not sure how to solve this, so we're going to try our answer choices. (If we knew how to solve it the straightforward way, we might do that first and then use the "trying the answer choices" strategy to check our work.)

We'll start with choice C, like we've been told to do.

That means we're supposing that there were originally 25 wives in the Yellow Tribe. Which means there are 75 in the Green Tribe. If the Green Tribe gives 15, they'll be down to 60 and the Yellow Tribe will be up to 40. Are those equal? Nope. Let's go smaller.

Choice B means that there are originally 20 in the Yellow Tribe, and 60 in the Green. When they do the exchange, that'll make 35 in the Yellow Tribe, and 45 in the Green. Closer.

Choice A says that the Yellow Tribe started with 15, which means the Green Tribe started with 45. Do the exchange, and the Yellow Tribe is up to 30, and the Green Tribe is down to . . . 30. There we go. **A** is right.

ERRONEOUS: WRONG

$\mathcal{E}x$. If $|x^2 - 6| \leq 30$, which of the following is the greatest possible value of x?

- A. −6
- B. −1
- C. 0
- D. 6
- E. 36

Solving inequalities can be tricky, unless you've recently studied for a test on them. The signs flip at unexpected moments. So let's not bother with algebra.

Normally we'd start by trying choice C, but this time we'll modify the rule. *If a problem calls for the greatest or least possible number, start by trying the greatest or least and then work down or up.* The reasoning is that, if the biggest (or least) number available works, we should go with that one and save a whole lot of work.

Since this problem calls for the greatest possible value, let's start by trying choice E, 36.

$|x^2 - 6| \leq 30$

If we make x equal to 36, the problem becomes $|(36)^2 - 6| \leq 30$

$|1296 - 6| \leq 30$

$|1290| \leq 30$ **? Nah. The absolute value of 1290 is a lot more than 30.**

Let's go down a notch to choice D:

$|6^2 - 6| \leq 30$

$|36 - 6| \leq 30$

$|30| \leq 30$. **Is thirty less than or equal to thirty?**

Sure is! D's our boy.

Occurred on the Job, Park Avenue at 70th Street:

Walked student with ailing hamster to Upper East Side vet. Hamster determined to either have congestive heart failure or a cough. Doctor gave him a $500 MRI. Diagnosis: a cough. Hamster survived.

Your Tutor Asks You to Stay Strong

Let's take a second to do a self-assessment. The next sixty-five pages or so are going to be nitty-gritty math rules—just the ones you really need to know, but still a good number of them. I'll try to keep it light, but it's still not going to be terribly fun. Make an extra effort to concentrate. Once you surface from these pages, you'll have made it through the most grueling part of the book.

That said, if you're the type to glaze over calculating a tip, and you know doing too much math will make you put this book down forever, make sure at least to take a look at the following sections:

Averages   (page 96)
Functions   (page 99)
Percents   (page 110)
Definitions (page 151)

But make it through as much of the rest as you can. Take breaks, eat plenty of cookies, drink plenty of milk, and intersperse sections with tracks of music.

You can do it.

Sundry Strategies

Ditzy Distance,
OR Honestly, Who Really Takes Trains from Town A to Town B Anymore?

Let's start with a classic. When the SAT gets spoofed in movies (which happens surprisingly often), these are always the problems you hear about. Train A leaves Springfield going 35 miles per hour, Train B leaves two hours later going 40 miles per hour, blah blah.

These classics are still on the test, though they don't appear as frequently as they once did. They're often easy, but in their harder incarnations they can be super-hard. Before we tackle distance, there's something we have to re-learn from second grade:

$D = r \times t$
Distance = rate × time

Ready? Let's go.

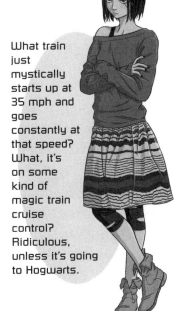

What train just mystically starts up at 35 mph and goes constantly at that speed? What, it's on some kind of magic train cruise control? Ridiculous, unless it's going to Hogwarts.

$\mathcal{E}x.$ If Marjorie crawls toward a branch that is 12 inches away at 3 inches per minute, and returns at 4 inches per minute, how long will the total trip take her? (By the way, Marjorie is a slug.)

We'll do the trip there first.

$D = r \times t$
$12 = 3(\text{inches per minute}) \times t$
$12/3 = t$
$4 = t$

Now the way back:

$D = r \times t$
$12 = 4(\text{inches per minute}) \times t$
$12/4 = t$
$3 = t$

So the round trip takes $3 + 4$, or 7 minutes.

Now for the baddies. There are three varieties of hostile distance problems on the SAT.

#1 Distance Baddy: The Catching Up Problem

Ex. **An overpriced SAT tutor leaves a student's house at 3:30 P.M., walking at 5 mph. If the student notices at 5 P.M. that her tutor has left his bag, and runs after him (aww) at 8 mph, at what time will the student overtake her tutor?**

This would be easy if the tutor stopped moving once his student started, but he's still moving away as she runs toward him. First we have to find the head-start distance, or how far the tutor has gone by the time his student notices that he's left his stuff. He's been going 5 mph for 1.5

hours, so he's made it 7.5 miles away (I live downtown, so that's approximately right, though why I didn't just take the subway is anyone's guess).

Now we subtract the lesser rate of speed from the greater, and get $8 - 5 = 3$ mph. This represents the speed at which the student is *gaining* on her tutor.

Now we just plug into $D = r \times t$ and solve.

$$\textbf{7.5 miles} = \textbf{3 mph} \times t$$
$$\textbf{2.5} = t$$

It will take 2.5 hours, so that means the student will catch up to her tutor at 7:30 P.M., at which point I hope he buys her a cupcake to compensate for her troubles.

#2 Distance Baddy: Average Speed

$\mathcal{E}x$. **If you fly to the moon at 200 mph and return at 300 mph, what is your average rate of speed?**

"Ah-ha!" you say. "It's halfway between. I say 250 miles an hour!"

But you're wrong. You'd have been suspicious, too, because a problem this hard would have appeared at the end of a section, which means that, statistically, most students get it wrong. It shouldn't be as easy as 250.

In SAT land, "overtake" means to catch up, not pull ahead.

The reason the answer isn't 250 mph is that you're spending more time going 200 mph than 300 mph, so your answer should be slightly closer

"Average Speed" Problem Steps:

1. Assign a distance.
2. Solve for the time each trip takes.
3. Plug round-trip distance and round-trip time into $D = r \times t$, and solve.

to 200 than 300. But, while utterly fascinating, that tidbit won't get us into Penn State.

Remember what to do when a problem bowls you over? That's right, consider plugging in numbers or trying answer choices. I didn't give you answer choices (let's say this problem was a grid-in), so we'll plug in numbers.

How are we supposed to know the distance to the moon? Oh well, let's make something up. A multiple of 200 and 300 will make our lives easier, so let's pick 600 miles. It's a little close to the Earth, but that's the astronomers' problem.

So, the trip there:

$600 = 200 \times t$

$3 = t$

And the trip back:

$600 = 300 \times t$

$2 = t$

So, for the round trip, we went 1200 miles in 5 hours.

$1200 = r \times 5$

$240 = r$

The average rate of speed is 240 mph, not 250 mph. Weird.

600 miles!!! Preposterous. The Moon wouldn't stay in orbit, it would just . . . oh God. The Moon just crashed into the Earth. Repeat, the Moon just crashed into the Earth.

EXONERATE: CLEAR OF BLAME

#3 Distance Baddy: Varying Rates

This kind has occurred with increasing frequency lately. It's another easy-seeming problem that's actually pretty rough.

$\mathcal{E}x$. **If Ex–President Bush drives from his house to the convenience store at 50 mph and returns at 70 mph, and the round trip takes six hours, how far away is the convenience store from his house?**

If you have know-it-all parents or siblings, try giving them this deceptively hard problem as you pass the salad bowl at dinner. Ha!

Once again, it seems we don't have enough info. How long did each trip take? They're both mushed together. Huh. Hard stuff.

Getting there:

$$D = 50 \times t_2$$

We have two variables and only one equation, which means we don't have enough information to work with. The return trip:

$$D = 70 \times t_2$$

Hmm. Since both trips have the same distance, at least we know that $50 \times t_1 = 70 \times t_2$.

We have one equation with two variables, so we don't have enough info to solve.

We also know, though, that the time it takes Bush to go to the convenience store and return is six hours.

Varying Rates Steps:
1. Set $r_1 \times t_1$ equal to $r_2 \times t_2$.
2. Make t_1 and t_2 add up to total time.
3. Use substitution to solve for t_1 or t_2.
4. Plug into corresponding original equation to get distance.

So $t_1 + t_2 = 6$.

That means $6 - t_2 = t_1$, so let's substitute:

$$50 \times (6 - t_2) = 70 \times t_2$$
$$300 - 50t_2 = 70t_2$$
$$300 = 120t_2$$
$$2.5 = t_2$$

It took George 2.5 hours to drive back. Two and a half hours at 70 mph means that, if

$$70 \times 2.5 = \text{Distance}$$
$$175 \text{ miles} = \text{the distance to the convenience store}$$

This one was complex, so try another on your own:

Ex. **If a snake slithers to a mouse hole at 4 mph and then, fattened, returns at 1 mph, and his total travel time is 12.5 hours, how far away is the mouse hole?**

Answer: 10 miles

Abbreviated Averages

Ah, averages. Another classic. You were fluent in averages, back when you were playing Pokémon and eating boogers. Now, seven years later, they're back with a vengeance. In fact, averages are one of the most common question types on the test.

Have you zoned out? This material's getting very technical. Go take a break, or skip to the next section and come back here later.

FACILE: EASY

Let's start with a few (at least vaguely) familiar definitions.

Mean: Classic average; add up and divide by the number of numbers. (The average of {1, 2, 2, 3, 4, and 5} is 17/6, or 2.8$\overline{3}$.)

Median: The middle number, when the numbers are listed in order. If you have an even number of numbers, average the middle two. (The median of {1, 2, 2, 3, 4, and 5} is 2.5.)

Mode: The most frequently occurring number. If no one number is more common than any other, the series is said to have multiple modes. (The mode of {1, 2, 2, 3, 4, and 5} is 2; the modes of {1, 1, 2, and 3, 3} are 1 and 3.)

Working with mode is rarely rough; you just have to rememorize its definition. Median has a tricky incarnation that can occur on the SAT:

Ex. **What is the least possible value of x, if the median of 400, 510, 420, 560, and x is x?**

First we have to put our numbers in order. And of course there's an x somewhere. If x is the median, it must be in the middle, so the sequence must look like this:

{400, 420, x, 510, 560}

The least value of x? It can't leave the center, so it must be somewhere from 420 to 510. So . . . 421? Nope. *Unless the problem says so, there's no reason x can't have the same value as a number already listed.* So the least possible value of x is **420**.

That's as bad as medians get. Mean, though, can be downright mean (heh, heh). When averages get hard, keep in mind something I like to call *average equivalency*:

Say you're told that four numbers average to 75. If it helps you puzzle through the problem, you might as well imagine that all the numbers actually *are* 75.

it's impossible to say "equivalency" aloud without sounding like a total geek. go ahead and try it. and see if you're not inspired to push a pair of phantom spectacles farther up your nose.

$\mathcal{Ex}$. If your author's average score after ten ratings on www.AmIHot .com is 3.4, what must his next rating be to have an average of 3.5?

Let's say that all 10 ratings so far have been precisely 3.4.

$$\frac{3.4 + 3.4 + 3.4 + 3.4 + 3.4 + 3.4 + 3.4 + 3.4 + 3.4 + 3.4 + x}{11} = 3.5$$

Author's Note:

This example is, of course, purely hypothetical.

$$3.4(10) + x = 3.5 \times 11$$
$$34 \times x = 38.5$$
$$x = 4.5$$

$\mathcal{Ex}$. If ten kittens weigh an average of 8 lbs. each, and a toddler from the backwoods named Kitten weighs 52 lbs., what is the average weight of all the creatures?

We're going to say that all the kittens weigh precisely 8 lbs. each.

$$\frac{10(8) + 1(52)}{(10 + 1)} = a$$
$$80 + 52 = 11a$$
$$132 = 11a$$
$$12 = a$$

FORGERY: FAKERY

Foiled Attempts to Cheat the SAT in Recent History

When you have one test with such high stakes attached, it's inevitable that cheaters will get creative.

COMMONPLACE:
- Sharing answers during breaks.
- Working on earlier sections using extra time from a later section.

RARER:
- Downloading vocab lists into a graphing calculator.
- Two friends take Subject Tests in reverse order and share answers during a break.

CRAZY:
- Printing vocab and formulas on the inside labels of water bottles.
- Once some kid apparently set up a business in which a guy took the test on the East Coast, left during the first break, and phoned the vocab words to a friend on the West Coast, who silkscreened them onto pencils from a van in the parking lot and sold them to test takers for $100 a pop.

I bring this up because it's funny to see how far people will go to avoid just preparing for the damn test. Do not try any of the above. If you were caught cheating, the repercussions would be catastrophic. If that's not enough, cheating on the SAT will make you feel like crap, if not now then later in life.

Fracked-up Functions

Your tutor is about to have a whole lot of fun with this book's typesetters. That's because these are the kinds of problems with all the crazy symbols. You know, stuff like:

Ex. If $x \xi y = x + 5y^2$, then what is $4 \xi 2$?

These problems aren't actually too hard, I promise. The reason so many students get them wrong is that they're scary to look at. You can easily think, "I've never seen a ξ before! Everyone else got taught that, and I've never seen it!" And that's the kind of thinking that can get you in trouble. Don't worry—no one's seen a weird symbol like ξ before;

FRENETIC: FRANTIC

it's made up just for the question. Choke back your panic and you'll see it's not so hard. Just play hostage and do exactly as they tell you.

They've defined a function. All this problem is saying is that if you have "something" ξ "something else," you do what they tell you to those things. In the above case:

$4 \xi 2$
means $4 + 5(2)^2$
Which is 24.
That's it! See, not so bad.

You'll find these are just like functions ("$f(x)$"), which you might have studied in precalculus. A more straightforward function problem looks something like this:

Ex. If $f(x) = (x-3)^2 - 2x$, what is $f(-2)$?
Same thing as before. Plug -2 in for x in the function.
$(-2-3)^2 - 2(-2)$
$(-5)^2 + 4$
29.

Functions can also appear in graph form:

When a function is graphed, the y-axis (vertical) represents the result when the value on the x-axis (horizontal) is put into an equation.

On the SAT you might have a function graphed for which you never learn the equation.

FUTILE: USELESS

$\mathcal{E}x$. **In the graph above, what is $f(1)$?**

We have to analyze the graph to determine the answer (and who doesn't like analyzing graphs!). What the question is really asking for is the y value when x is 1. According to the graph, where x is 1, y is 0. So the answer is **0**.

Other ways a question like this might be phrased:

If $f(x) = -2$, what is x?

(In this case, we need to determine what the x value is when the y-value is -2. Looks like it's $\approx$ **0.5.**)

What is $f(f(2))$?

(Just work through each part individually, starting with the center. $f(2) = 0$, so now we have to find $f(0)$, which is **0**.)

Caustic Combinations and Pungent Permutations

Combinations can be rough, because there's a good chance you've never seen them before. Unless you've been dabbling in college-level statistics and logic courses, you should listen up. (And if you have: wow.)

There are two new concepts to worry about, *combinations* and *permutations*, both of which (whew) are handily resolved by your calculator.

Combinations

These require you to find out how many variations of a situation are possible.

Ex. **If Sharice has been asked to the prom by nine different boys, but can only say yes to two, how many possibilities are there for the pair of boys that Sharice will accept?**

Math purists will swear on a formula for combinations that looks as follows:

Ignore this formula! Down with formulas!

$$n \text{ take } k: \frac{n!}{k!(n-k)!} \quad \frac{9!}{2!(9-2)!} = 36$$

But you shouldn't do that.

Your calculator will solve it for you, via a fancy-sounding function called "nCr." Yes, you'll be using one of those weird buttons that you've always wished played mp3s.

If Sharice has 9 boys to choose from, and will take only 2, just press 9 nCr 2 (9 "take" 2). You get **36**. And that's your answer.

Try these:

1. You own a firm that employs 8 different obese chimney sweeps. If you are sending 3 out on a job, how many teams are possible?

2. If there are 60 different cow documentaries available to purchase, and you can buy only two, how many possibilities are possible for your new cow documentary collection?

3. If 4 of the 20 students in a class are to be given Jaguars, how many groups of lucky recipients are possible?

As long as they mean Jaguar the car.

Answers:
1. 8 nCr 3=56
2. 60 nCr 2=1770
3. 20 nCr 4=4845

Permutations

While combinations are "grab bag" problems, which worked like you were plucking things out of a bag, in *permutations* "order matters"—or, in other words, what you're choosing will be arranged in a specific configuration.

Let's check back in with Sharice.

Ex. **Let's say she's got the same nine boys clamoring for her attention at the prom, but this time she's decided she's going to take one boy to the prom and a different boy to the after-prom party. How many possibilities are there for her company for the evening?**

Set up a couple of blanks on your paper:

—— ——

These represent the possibilities for her two dates—the first is her prom date, the second her party date. Let's start with the first. How many boys does she have to choose from for her primary date? Nine.

<u>9</u> ——

Now how many are left for the secondary spot? We've already placed one boy, so there are eight left.

<u>9</u> <u>8</u>

Now we just multiply our blanks. $9 \times 8 = 72$. There are **72** possibilities.

SCIENTIFIC CALCULATORS: locate nCr as either a standalone button, or a "2nd" function to another button.

GRAPHING CALCULATORS: nCr can generally be found in the "Math" menu, under "probability."

By the way, the SAT will allow you to use just about any standard calculator you would use in school. The exceptions are calculators with keyboards, or those that make noise. Xbox 360s—also not allowed. Check www.ets.org for full details.

Ex. **If Becky owns 10 Daniel Radcliffe posters, but has room on her wall for only 4, how many arrangements are possible?**

First, we'll set up our four blanks to represent the four spots on the wall:

___ ___ ___ ___

There are 10 posters available for the first spot, then 9 for the second, then 8, then 7.

$$\underline{10} \times \underline{9} \times \underline{8} \times \underline{7} = 5040$$

Ex. **Five embezzling pandas are to be arranged in a police line-up. If the fattest panda must be in the middle, how many lineups are possible?**

We'll place the fat panda first. There's only one possibility for him, so:

___ ___ $\underline{1}$ ___ ___

Now let's fill in the other four. There are four bears left for the first slot, then three for the second, etc.

$$\underline{4} \times \underline{3} \times \underline{1} \times \underline{2} \times \underline{1} = 24$$

Ex. *Modification to previous problem:* **Five embezzling pandas are to be arranged in a police lineup. If the two skinniest pandas must be on either end, how many lineups are possible?**

Five slots: ___ ___ ___ ___ ___

Let's place the skinny ones first. There are two skinny pandas, and each can be on either end

When in doubt on probability problems, multiply.

So that means we have two available for our left slot, and only one remaining for our right slot.

  2 ___ ___ ___ 1

Now we can fill in the remaining three pandas:

  2 × 3 × 2 × 1 × 1 = **12**

Now let's let the pandas get really *crazy*! Aren't we having fun?!

Ex. *Modification:* **Five embezzling pandas are to be arranged in a police lineup. If the fattest panda must be in the middle and the two skinniest pandas must be on either end, how many lineups are possible?**

Placing the fat panda in his obligatory center position, we get:

  ___ ___ 1 ___ ___

Now we'll place the two skinnies.

  2 ___ 1 ___ 1

tutors tend to phrase things annoyingly like that.

And then fill in the two remaining (apparently ideal bodyweight) pandas.

  2 × 2 × 1 × 1 × 1 = **4** possibilities.

Note: Combinations and Permutations can easily be altered into probability problems. Don't fret; just make the result of the combination or permutation the denominator of the probability. For example . . .

Ex. **If five equally-matched sumo wrestlers named Rose, Gertrude, Annabelle, Melrose, and Delores are in an archery competition, what is the chance that Annabelle will come in first and Gertrude second?**

First, we'll find out how many possibilities there are for first and second place:

$$\underline{5} \times \underline{4} = 20$$

The probability of any one case happening is just one of those 20, or **1/20**.

Improbable Probability, OR What's with All These Marble Problems?

Which leads us into our next topic.

Apparently, the SAT's probability question writer was prevented from playing marbles as a kid. Whatever the sob story, the SAT has an obsession with round globes of glass. Invariably, they're in a few different colors, and someone's pulling them at random from a bag. *Who does that?*

"GEEK!"

In fact, probability problems are classic examples of what I call "geek problems," whose existence hinges on some hypothetical person doing something *très* geeky.

If something's sure to happen (ex: child star entering rehab), its probability is 1. If it'll never happen (ex: a date with Giselle), the probability is 0. All other probabilities fall somewhere in between.

Ex. Eugene has constructed a wheel on which he has written the months of the year. Each time he spins it, it finishes on a random month. What is the probability that it will stop on a month beginning with "M"?

Probability is always:

$$\frac{number\ of\ correct\ options}{total\ options}$$

In this case, since there are two months beginning with "M," March and May, out of twelve total months, the probability is 2/12, or **1/6**.

If more than one event has to occur, *simply multiply the probability of each event.* For example:

Ex. What is the chance of rolling a 1, then an even number, then a prime number, on three tosses of a six-sided die?

The chance of rolling a 1 is 1/6, an even number (2, 4, 6) is 3/6, and a prime number (2, 3, 5) is 3/6. Multiply all the probabilities and you get 9/216, or **1/24**.

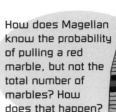

How does Magellan know the probability of pulling a red marble, but not the total number of marbles? How does that happen?

Ex. Magellan holds a bag containing red, purple, blue, and white marbles. If his chance of randomly pulling out a red marble is $\frac{1}{3}$, his chance of pulling out a purple marble is $\frac{1}{4}$, his chance of pulling out a blue marble is $\frac{1}{12}$, and there are 60 white marbles, how many marbles does Magellan hold in his bag?

IMPARTIAL/NONPARTISAN: UNBIASED

Let's find out the *chance* of pulling out a white marble. To start, we can add the chances of pulling out the other three colors ($\frac{1}{3} + \frac{1}{4} + \frac{1}{12}$), and find out that there's an $\frac{8}{12}$, or $\frac{2}{3}$, chance of *not* pulling white. That means there must be a ($1 - \frac{2}{3}$, or) $\frac{1}{3}$ chance of pulling white.

I like marbles!

1 white marble for every 3 marbles means:

$$\frac{1 \text{ white marble}}{3 \text{ marbles}} = \frac{60 \text{ white marbles}}{x \text{ marbles}}$$

Solve by cross-multiplying.

60 white marbles for every 180 marbles

Railing Against Ratios

Ratios are a particularly devious concept for the SAT to trot out, since they look easy but actually go against everything else you've been taught. You've been lulled into assuming that mathematical relationships are generally parts to whole. "Forty percent of the students" and "three-fifths of the pie," for example, describe portions of the whole. Ratios are part to *part*, which is why they can trip you up. The jerks.

$\mathcal{E}x$. **If an animal farm raises singing glowworms and burping spiders in a 7:2 ratio, and there are 189 animals total, how many glowworms are there?**

IMPEDE: BLOCK

First thing, we have to find out how much 7 *plus* 2 is . . . 9. Now we can treat the problem like a normal proportion:

$$\frac{7 \text{ glowworms}}{9 \text{ animals total}} = \frac{g \text{ glowworms}}{189 \text{ animals total}}$$

By cross-multiplying, we find that $9g = 1323$, so $g = \mathbf{147}$.

Ex. **If Grandma Madge's extra-special chocolate chip cookies require flour, mustard, and chocolate chips in a 10:7:3 ratio, how many pounds of chocolate chips are required to make 7.5 pounds of cookies?**

Mmm . . . chocolate chip cookies

Let's get the total for the ratio first. $10 + 7 + 3 = 20$.

$$\frac{3 \text{ lbs. chips}}{20 \text{ lbs. total}} = \frac{c \text{ lbs. chips}}{7.5 \text{ lbs. total}}$$

Cross-multiply, and we find $22.5 = 20c$, so $c = 22.5/20$, or **1.125** lbs. of chips.

Comparing Ratios

You might also be called on to compare ratios.

INADVERTENTLY: ACCIDENTALLY

Ex. If A:B is 2:11, and B:C is 5:4, what is A:C?

You *can't* directly compare A and C and decide that it must be 2:4. What you first have to do is to make your Bs equivalent. Doing so is going to feel a lot like finding a common denominator back when you were adding fractions and playing PS1.

A:B = 2:11 (×5) = 10:55
B:C = 5:4(×11) = 55:44

So A:C = 10:44, which can be reduced to **5:22**.

Ex. **If the giraffe to hippo ratio is 1:7, and the hippo to doberman ratio is 1:7, what is the giraffe to doberman ratio?**
G:H = 1:7(×1) = 1:7
H:D = 1:7(×7) = 7:49, so G:D = 1:49

Poof! Percents

This one we can blow out of the water quickly. You were once a pro at these . . . of course, you were nine.

You'll face two varieties of percent problems.

An excellent issue, by the way, if only for the articles.

Percent Change

Ex. **If you bought a copy of *National Geographic's Lifestyles of the Cave Roach* for $40 and resold it for $52, what percent higher was the resale price?**

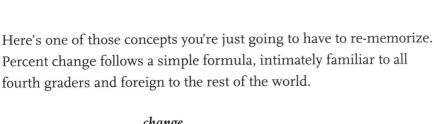

Here's one of those concepts you're just going to have to re-memorize. Percent change follows a simple formula, intimately familiar to all fourth graders and foreign to the rest of the world.

$$\text{Percent Change} = \frac{change}{original}$$

The change in price is $12, so therefore the resale price is $\frac{12}{40}$ higher, or (as our trusty calculator informs us) 0.3 higher. Since *decimals are converted to percents by shifting the decimal point two places to the right*, 0.3 is equal to 30%.

Percent Translation

Ex. **35 percent of 60 is what percent of 42?**

   a. 35   d. 60

   b. 40   e. 200

   c. 50

Finding 35% of 60 isn't too tricky—but finding it as a percentage of 42 is.

If your instincts tell you to solve through a proportion, go ahead—but the very easiest way is through a sleight-of-hand I call *percent translation*. Simply memorize the following equivalent terms:

"percent"	*means*	÷ 100
"of"	*means*	×
"is"	*means*	=
"what"	*means*	*y*

And mindlessly translate the problem into algebra.

"35 percent of 60 is what percent of 42?" means

$$35 \div 100 \times 60 = y \div 100 \times 42$$

$$21 = \frac{y}{100} \times 42$$

$$2100 = 42y$$

$$50 = y$$

Answer choice **C**.

Just memorize the translation. This approach requires only four brain cells, and works every time.

Malicious Mixtures

Mixtures are a genre of problem that involves combining huge amounts of manly things like gravel or sand, and will be very helpful if you plan to go into construction.

Ex. **If 15% of a 200-gallon mixture is alcohol, and 70 gallons of alcohol are added, what percent of the new mixture is alcohol?**

First, let's find out exactly how much of this mysterious (and assuredly scientific) solution is alcohol. 15% of 200 means 15/100×200, which equals 30. So right now we have:

$$\frac{30 \text{ gallons alcohol}}{200 \text{ gallons total}}$$

Now we'll pour in the additional alcohol. This will change the amount of alcohol, *but will also increase the total.*

someone planning a party?

$$\frac{30 \text{ gallons alcohol} + 70}{200 \text{ gallons total} + 70} = \frac{100 \text{ gallons alcohol}}{270 \text{ gallons total}} \approx .37, \text{ or } 37\%$$

Ex. Currently, 155 of Bjorn's 395 marbles are yellow. How many yellow marbles should he remove if he wants his probability of randomly choosing a yellow marble to be $\frac{1}{3}$?

a. 0   d. 32
b. 15   e. 35
c. 30

Set up a similar equation as last time, part over whole:

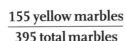

$$\frac{155 \text{ yellow marbles}}{395 \text{ total marbles}}$$

The amount we're going to take away is a mystery, so we'll make it *x*. The key thing, as with the last problem, is

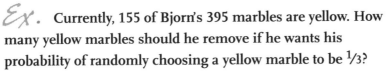

This problem is a great candidate for trying answer choices—just start with C and see if it works, then go higher or lower until you find the right answer. But we're also going to try the straightforward way.

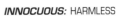

INNOCUOUS: HARMLESS

to remember that if you're going to take away some yellow marbles, you're going to affect the total, too. So:

$$\frac{155\,\text{yellow marbles} - x}{395\,\text{total marbles} - x} = \frac{1}{3}$$

Cross-multiplying gives us:

$$3(155 - x) = 395 - x$$
$$465 - 3x = 395 - x$$
$$465 = 395 + 2x$$
$$70 = 2x$$
$$35 = x$$

Choice **E** is correct.

Lingering Long Division

Long division?! [Groan]

That's right, there are problems on the SAT that call for long division. Call them *Third Grade II: The Revenge.*

But I *love* long division!

Ex. **If the remainder when *r* is divided by 14 is 3, and the remainder when *s* is divided by 14 is 2, what is the remainder when *rs* is divided by 14?**

Remainders?! Surely I'm kidding, right? Alas, I'm not.

Since we know we should plug in numbers when in doubt, let's assign values to *r* and *s*. The *r* has to equal something that has 3 left

INTEMPERATE: EXTREME

What Your Six-year-old Brother Should Be Doing to Prepare

Ideally, if we were all raised by Ph.D. parents with a distaste for television and a knack for discussing Venn diagrams at the dinner table, we wouldn't have to prepare for the SAT. But instead, we spent too much time playing kickball and have to scramble our way through a snarky guide that tells us how to pretend to be that perfect nerd kid.

Well, take a long look at your younger sibling. Wouldn't it be nice to prevent him from having to work so hard in the end game? There are a few early seeds you can plant that will make him a damn good natural test taker.

Let's be honest. All my tips to get a better score on the Critical Reading and Writing sections, while effective, are essentially fakery; they're ways to perform above your natural reading level. If you can raise your reading level, then you'll have less need for the tricks. That's hard to do in the short term, but it's not too late for your younger sibling. If he's young enough, *read to him*. If he's older than that, just *make sure he's reading*. It doesn't matter if it's comic books, Harry Potter, magazines, massive quantities of cereal boxes. Whatever. Just keep him taking in language.

As for math, there's something in the Math sections test that only rarely shows up in middle school/high school curricula: logic and reasoning. So go on eBay and buy a 1970s-era college logic textbook for a buck and tell little bro that he has to read twenty pages of it a week for his whole eighth-grade summer vacation. Sure, he'll be yelling and screaming, but if you get your parents on board, then suddenly you look like a star and you have your younger sibling out of your hair for a nice long time. You can even go further and suggest he take a logic course at the local junior college. (He might like that, actually, because he'll be a hit with the college girls.)

TEXTBOOK OF LOGIC

A. WOLF

Take a look at this 1962 beauty. Little bro is guaranteed to hate you for all time.

over when it's divided by 14; *(after a brief hair-pulling session)* 17 works, because 14 goes in it once, with 3 left over. Likewise, *s* could be 16. Okay, *rs* has to be 17×16, or 272. Cool!

Now we just have to divide 272 by 14. *(after a second with calculator)* Damn. It says 19.42857143. That doesn't give us an answer.

The key to doing remainders on your calculator is to subtract the whole number away first, then multiply by what you divided by. In other words,

INTUITIVE: INSTINCTIVE

to find the remainder we'll have to multiply 0.42857143 by 14. Which is **6**, our answer.

Ex. **What is the remainder when 300 is divided by 23?**

1. $300 \div 23 = 13.04347826$
2. $13.04347826 - 13 = 0.04347826$
3. $0.04347826 \times 23 = 1$

"FOIL," as everyone knows, stands for "First, Outer, Inner, Last," and tells us how $(x+7)(2x-1)$ comes out to be $2x^2-x+14x-7$, or $2x^2+13x-7$.

Polymorphed Polynomials (OR, Forced Factoring and FOILing)

At least you've had to deal with polynomials recently, so we won't be taxing the elementary school memory centers of your brain any longer.

This is one area in which the SAT is very predictable. If you see something that looks like you can factor it, do it. If you think you can FOIL it, do that. Just go on autopilot.

Ex. **If $4x^2+3x+1=2$, and x is positive, what is the value of x?**

First we have to get all our values on one side, equal to zero on the other side. By subtracting 4 from both sides we get:

$$4x^2+3x-1=0$$

INUNDATE: FLOOD

We factor the equation to get:

$$(4x-1)(x+1)=0$$

This means:

$$4x-1=0 \ \text{OR} \ x+1=0$$
$$4x=1 \qquad x=-1$$
$$x=1/4$$

Since the problem stated that x was positive, its value has to be ¼.

$\mathcal{Ex}.$ **If $(x-6)$ is a factor of $x^2+10x+k$, what is the value of k?**

This equation looks like it can be factored, so let's do it.

$$x^2+10x+k=(x)(x).$$

Hmm . . . we're told that one of the factors has to be $(x-6)$, so let's rewrite:

$$x^2+10x+k=(x-6)(x+\underline{}).$$

Now, −6 has to add with whatever's in the blank to equal 10. So the blank has to be 16.

Don't forget our earlier lesson on pages 79–80: If a problem asks you to solve for an expression (ex. $x-y$), solve for that expression rather than for the individual variables.

INVECTIVE: INSULT

$$x^2 + 10x + k = (x-6)(x+16).$$

Our rules say that we should factor or FOIL whenever we can, so let's FOIL the expression $(x-6)(x+16)$, even if we're not sure why we're doing it.

$$x^2 + 10x + k = x^2 + 10x - 96$$

Whoa! Look at that. Now we see that $k = -96$.

What about those hard polynomials I've seen in class? you wonder. *The ones that need the quadratic formula?*

Truth is you won't need the quadratic formula for the SAT, though you will need it for the Math I and II subject tests (see page 15). It finds the roots of a polynomial, but whenever you have to use it I'd recommend actually using a graphing calculator program called QUADFORM. Either download it from a friend or online, or program the following into your Texas Instruments calculator:

```
PROGRAM: QUADFORM
:ClrHome
:Disp "QUADRATIC FORMULA"
:Prompt A,B,C

:B² – 4AC → D
:(–B + √ (D))/(2A) → R
:(–B – √ (D))/(2A) → S

:Disp "THE ROOTS ARE"
:Disp R, S
```

(Note: The → is what appears when you press "=" on your calculator while programming.)

INVETERATE/CHRONIC: HABITUAL

Un-expected Exponents

A *negative* exponent is just like a normal one, except you stick the result under 1. For example:

$$x^{-5} = 1/x^5$$
$$4^{-2} = 1/4^2, \text{ or } 0.0625$$

You can type them into your calculator just as you would a positive exponent, and get the correct result. Try calculating 4 ^ (−2) and see if you don't get 0.0625.

A *fractional* exponent is more complicated. The denominator stipulates the root of the equation, while the numerator expresses the power inside.

$$x^{3/2} = \sqrt{x^3}$$
$$x^{4/5} = \sqrt[5]{x^4}$$

Or, they can both go together:

$$x^{-1/4} = 1/\sqrt[4]{x}$$

It's okay if these continue to confuse you. Just remember—you can perform any operation on weird exponents that you would on any other exponent. Type it all into your calculator and let Texas Instruments sort it out.

While We're at It: Converting Decimals to Fractions

Most scientific and graphing calculators have functions that easily allow you to convert decimals to fractions. On the TI-83, for example, press MATH and select ▶FRAC

IRREPROACHABLE: BLAMELESS

Exponent Rules

$a^b \times a^c = a^{(b+c)}$

$(a^b)^c = a^{bc}$

$\dfrac{a^b}{a^c} = a^{(b-c)}$

$\mathcal{Ex}.$ If $\dfrac{x^{3/4}}{x^{1/2}}$ is equal to 3, what is x?

When you're dividing numbers with exponents, you subtract the exponents, so

$$\frac{x^{3/4}}{x^{1/2}} = x^{1/4}.$$

If $x^{1/4} = 3$, we can raise both sides to the fourth power to get rid of the exponent:

$(x^{1/4})^4 = 3^4$, so $x = 81$.

$\mathcal{Ex}.$ If $(x^{-2/3})^{-2} = y^{1/5}$, what is the value of y, ~~in terms of x?~~

A. $x^{1/5}$ D. x^5

B. x E. x^{20}

C. $x^{20/3}$

Multiplying the powers on the left leaves you with:
$x^{4/3} = y^{1/5}$

Raise both sides to the fifth power to get plain old y:

$(x^{4/3})^5 = (y^{1/5})^5$

$x^{20/3} = y$, or choice C.

Don't forget to cross out "in terms of" phrases; they don't mean anything.

Soporific Sequences

You can solve a sequence problem without having to think too hard if you also happen to have a spare half hour. They're a tease: Either do brainless work for a hell of a long time, or think harder for less. We're going to opt for thinking harder for less time, if only because that means we can nap for longer afterward.

Ex. **In the following repeating sequence, what is the 903rd item?**

Ж,♣,✿,♂,☻,Ж,♣,✿,♂,☻ . . .

Is that a dark elf smiley-face?

We could count out 903 symbols. But then we wouldn't have time for the rest of the section, and we'd never get to take Intro to Nude Figure Drawing in college. Hmm . . . just follow my directions instead.

How many symbols go by before the sequence starts to repeat? Five. Divide 903 by 5.

Did you get 180.6? Not good enough. I need a remainder. (If you're not sure how to get one, look back on page 114.)

The remainder, 3, tells us how far into the sequence we need to count. We want the third symbol, or ✿.

Ex. **What is the 328th symbol in the same sequence?**

GEEK!

328/4=82 even, with no remainder.
So the answer is the last symbol in the sequence, or ☻.

Steps:

1. Count how many terms go by before repeating.
2. Divide requested term by that value.
3. The remainder tells you how far to count into the sequence (if there is no remainder, use the last term in the sequence).

Winky Work Problems

Work problems generally involve multiple things working together to accomplish a task, and (bizarrely) almost always involve pool pumps.

Ex. **If Pump A can fill a pool in 3 hours, and Pump B takes 7 hours to fill the same pool, how long will it take them to fill the pool when they're working together?**

Okay, we might feel stumped for a moment, which means we turn to our "I'm screwed" solution: plugging in numbers. We'll make up a number of gallons for the pool. A multiple of 3 and 7 will be handy, so let's go with . . . 210 gallons (eek, it's small: don't dive into this pool). Pump A can spew 210 gallons in 3 hours, and since

work = rate × time,
$$210 = r \times 3,$$

so its rate is 70 gallons/hr.
As for Pump B, it can pump 210 gallons in 7 hours, which means

$$210 = r \times 7$$

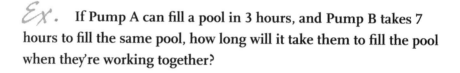

Who bought Pump B? It sucks.

Its rate is 30 gallons/hr.

What's their combined rate? $30 + 70$, or 100 gallons per hour. Working together:

$$210 = 100 \times t$$
$$2.1 = t$$

It will take both pumps, working together, **2.1 hours.**

Work problems can also be masquerading *inverse proportion* problems:

$\mathcal{E}x.$ **If it takes a family of four 2.5 hours to clean its house, how long would it take five people to do the same job, if everyone works at the same rate?**

You might be tempted to set up a proportion: 4 is to 2.5 as 5 is to . . . (*tap tap tap on the calculator . . .*) 3.125 hours. But does that make sense? Should it take 5 people *longer*? Nope. Common sense tells us the amount of time should go down.

In an inverse proportion, $xy = k$, *where* x *and* y *are the values in question and* k *is a constant.* So in this case, $4 \times 2.5 = 10$, which means $k = 10$. Now we're changing our x, so our equation becomes:

$$5 \times x = 10$$

$x = 2$. It would take two hours to clean the house with five people.

I like to think of k as the "man hours" a job requires. It represents how long it would take one person to do the job alone.

Let's try the same thing as a straightforward inverse proportion.

Ex. If *l* and *m* are inversely proportional, and *l* equals 20 when *m* equals 15, what does *l* equal when *m* is 3?

$lm = k$
$20 \times 15 = 300$ (now we know our constant, *k*, is 300)
$l \times 3 = 300$
$l = 100$.

The Victims of Venn

Venn diagrams are these cruel accumulations of circles that look like the Olympic rings as they'd appear in the nightmare of a math tutor. Or so I've heard.

I don't know who this Venn guy is, but his diagrams are helpful in problems asking you to compare two groups.

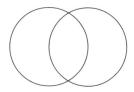

Um . . . John Venn was a British-born mathematician, 1834-1923. Duh.

Ex. If, out of 50 vampires, 36 suck preppies' blood and 34 suck punks' blood, at most how many suck only preppies' blood?

LAMENT: MOURN

First let's draw a Venn diagram and label the circles:

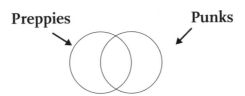

Now, write the number that belongs to each category below the labels, *but not inside the circles*, not yet.

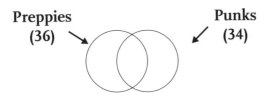

If all the vampires liked only preppies, or punks, but never both, that means we'd have (36 + 34) 70 vampires total. But we don't have 70, we have 50, which means that 20 have to exist in the middle category.

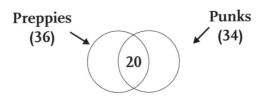

What remains of each circle will be for the *only* preppies and *only* punks categories, which are found by subtracting the middle number from the totals.

36 − 20 = 16, and

34 − 20 = 14, so:

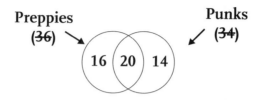

Preppies   **Punks**
(~~36~~)   (~~34~~)

16 (20) 14

Our question asked us how many liked *only* preppies, so the answer is **16**.

Try the following for practice:

Ex.   If, in a group of 81 mutant frogs, 70 are fuchsia and 51 have 3 or more legs, at least how many are both fuchsia and have 3 or more legs?

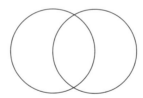

Answer: 40 frogs are fuchsia with 3 or more legs.

All About Angles

Ah, geometry. You'll find a good amount of it on your math sections, and it's a perfect way to lose a bunch of points if you're not prepared.

Ex. **If two sides of a triangle are formed by the radii of a circle, and the central angle is 82°, one of the triangle's other angle measurements could be:**

A. 48°   D. 83°

B. 49°   E. 164°

C. 82°

Let's draw our picture.

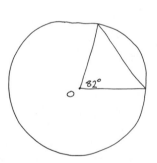

If two of the triangle's sides are radii, they must be equal (congruent), which means that the angles opposite them are also congruent.

> A ***central angle*** is an angle formed at the center of a circle.

LIVID: SUPER-MAD

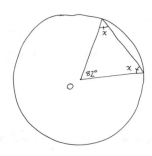

Since the interior angles of a triangle total 180°, we know that $82° + x° + x° = 180°$.

$2x = 98$

$x = 49$, or

Choice **B**.

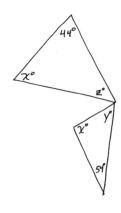

In the figure above, if $y = \frac{5}{6}z$, what is the value of x?

First Geometry Rule

If a problem doesn't give you a picture, draw one right away. It doesn't have to be pretty, just functional, like your first car.

Here, we'll have to use our awareness of angle relationships to construct a couple of equations. Within each triangle:

$x + z + 44 = 180$ **and** $x + y + 54 = 180$

Therefore we can set both expressions equal to each other:

$x + z + 44 = x + y + 54$ **(now subtract x and 44 from both sides)**
$z = y + 10$

As stated in the problem, we know that $\frac{5}{6} z = y$, so let's substitute that for y.

$z = \frac{5}{6} z + 10$
$\frac{1}{6} z = 10$
$z = 60$.

Substituting that into the first equation, we find:

$x + 60 + 44 = 180$
$x = 76$

Unless stated otherwise, you can assume that all figures provided on the SAT are drawn to scale.

Ex. **If a hexagon's interior angles are in a 4:5:6:8:8:9 ratio, what is the measure of its largest angle?**

First we need to know how to find the sum of the interior angles of a polygon. You have a couple of options:

1 Memorize (or program into your graphing calculator) the interior angles formula:

Sum of the interior angles of a polygon = $(n-2)$ 180, where n is its number of sides.

Or

2 You can just draw the figure and divide it into triangles (each of which contains 180°):

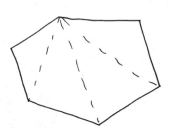

$$(4 \text{ triangles}) \times (180°) = 720°$$

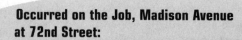

Occurred on the Job, Madison Avenue at 72nd Street:

An odd smell from student during weekly sessions that subsides over time as student grows comfortable. Tutor realizes: Student is a nervous farter.

Either way, we discover that the sum of the interior angles of a hexagon is 720°.

Now it's a straightforward ratio problem (for a review of ratios, see page 108).

$$4+5+6+8+8+9=40$$

The largest is 9 out of those 40, so the angle's measure is 9/40 of 720°, or **162°**.

The Perils of Parallel

Parallel lines are important on the SAT because they help us determine which angles are equal (or "congruent").

When two parallel lines are cut by a transversal, eight different angles are created, each with one of two angle measurements:

Keep on at it! Not too much more math to go.

LOATHE: HATE

So if you're given (or can solve for) the degree measure of any one angle, you can find all of the angles.

Ex.

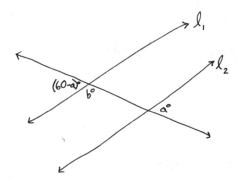

In the figure above, what is b equal to, if $l_1 \parallel l_2$?

Huh. We know which angles should be congruent. But that means a is equal to $60 - a$. Is that even possible? Try to find out:

$a = 60 - a$
$2a = 60$
$a = 30$

Whadya know? If $a = 30$, and b is supplementary to it, then b must equal **150°**. (By the way, it's impossible that a be equal to $a - 60$. But $a = 60 - a$ is totally feasible.)

Whether Scores Really Are Higher on the October Test

Some people think that if they take the SAT in October, they're in an easier pool, because a lot of slackers will be taking it last minute.

It's a good thought, but it's also wrong. There's no meaningful difference in score results between different test administrations. Same goes for Saturday versus Sunday tests. (Sunday test dates are available only to students who are unable to take the test on Saturday for religious reasons.)

Nefarious Number Lines

Once upon a time, you knew number lines as those things a bunny jumped on to teach you addition. (You remember, +2 meant two adorable hops to the right.)

Now, however, you can get number line problems that look like complicated gang graffiti:

Ex.

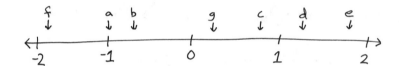

In the number line above, which letter corresponds to the value of *f*×*g*?

A. *a*   D. *d*

B. *b*   E. *e*

C. *c*

Just approximate the value of each letter. *f* looks like . . . let's say −1.8. And *g* looks like . . . how about ⅓? So *f*×*g*=−0.6. Which of these letters is closest to −0.6? **B.**

The other important thing to remember is that, on a number line, *the distance between two terms is the term on the right minus the term on the left.* So the distance between 4 and 20 is (20−4), or 16. The distance between −11.5 and 3.2 is (3.2−(−11.5)), or 14.7.

This concept may seem basic, but can be helpful in more complex problems, like the following:

Ex.

In the number line above, if the distance between X and Y is three more than the distance from Y to Z, what is the length of XZ?

Let's set up some equations.

The distance between X and Y is equal to $Y-X$, or $\frac{3}{a} - \frac{3}{2a}$.

The distance between Y and Z is equal to $Z-Y$, or $\frac{7}{2a} - \frac{3}{a}$.

Since we're told XY is three more than YZ, $\frac{3}{a} - \frac{3}{2a} = \frac{7}{2a} - \frac{3}{a} + 3$

$\frac{3}{a} - \frac{3}{2a} = \frac{7}{2a} - \frac{3}{a} + 3$ **(Multiply both sides by a to simplify things.)**

$3 - \frac{3}{2} = \frac{7}{2} - 3 + 3a$

$\frac{3}{2} = \frac{1}{2} + 3a$

$1 = 3a$

$1/3 = a$

$1/3 = a$. So our actual points are:

Therefore, the value of the distance from X to Z is $Z-X$, or $\frac{21}{2} - 9$, or $\frac{3}{2}$.

$\mathcal{E}x$. **If in ye olden times there were 7 leagues between Abel's home and Bathsheba's home, 20 leagues between Bathsheba's home and Cain's home, and 3 leagues between Cain's home and Daedelus's home, what was the difference between the maximum and minimum possible distances between Abel's home and Daedelus's home?**

Well, let's say the homes are in a straight line, and in the given order.

In this case, the distance between Abel and Daedelus is about as far as it can be. We add all the distances, and come up with 30 leagues for the maximum.

The minimum, however, is trickier. We'll have to manipulate the picture until we get A and D as close to each other as possible. Basically, we're going to take our straight line and fold it like a pool lounge chair, so that it looks like this:

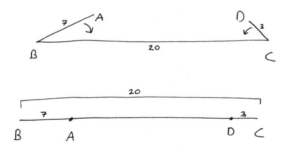

The distance between A and D is now $20 - 7 - 3$, or 10. So the difference between the maximum and minimum values of AD is $30 - 10$, or **20**.

Even if you're given points that are in alphabetical order, don't assume they have to exist in that order. It's one of the SAT's favorite tricks.

Look at Me, I'm So Cute, I'm Pythagorean!
OR, Righteous Right Triangles

The SAT definitely has a love affair with right triangles. And why not? They're sharp, they're elegant, and they don't smell.

For us, right triangles mean loads of Pythagorean theorem ($a^2 + b^2 = c^2$) calculations.

And where there are right triangles, there are the truly elite, Green Beret, special right triangles. Whenever you see any angle measuring 30°, 45°, or 60°, you'd better bet you've got a special right triangle on your hands (or potentially, in the case of 60°, an equilateral triangle). Their angles are listed at the beginning of each Math section, but you'll be using them so frequently that I'd suggest memorizing them:

45 – 45 – 90:

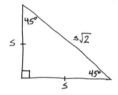

30 – 60 – 90:

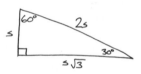

These come up in unexpected places, such as . . .

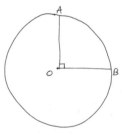

If the area of the circle above with center O is 49π, what is the distance between points A and B?

Pythagorean Theorem

$$a^2 + b^2 = c^2$$

Which means that, in a right triangle, the sum of the squares of the two sides is equal to the square of the hypotenuse.

First, let's find out the radius. Since 49π is the area, and the area of a circle is πr^2, then $r = 7$. If we make a triangle, we find that (and here's a concept you'll see come up again and again), since two of its sides are radii, it's an isosceles triangle.

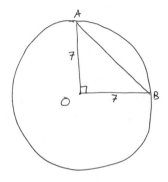

An **isosceles triangle** has two sides that are equal.

An **equilateral triangle** has three sides that are equal.

A **right triangle** has one angle of 90°.

A **Bermuda triangle** sinks planes and ships.

An isosceles right triangle has two congruent angles, which makes this one a 45–45–90 special triangle. So we know that the hypotenuse is $\sqrt{2} \times$ a side, or in this case $7\sqrt{2}$.

The **area of a circle** is πr^2

The **circumference of a circle** is $2\pi r$.

Equilateral triangles should automatically lead, in your mind, to 30–60–90 triangles.

$\mathcal{E}x.$ **If the perimeter of an equilateral triangle is 30, what is its area?**

Since we aren't given a picture, first thing we do is draw one. Since all sides are equal, they must each be 10:

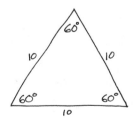

MELANCHOLY: SAD

We'll need to drop an altitude if we hope to find the area, at which point the picture will look like this:

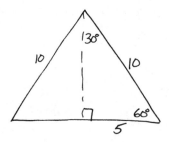

Aha! A 30–60–90 triangle on the right. The hypotenuse is two times the shortest side. That means the dotted-line side must be $5\sqrt{3}$. Since the area of a triangle is $\frac{1}{2} \times$ base $\times$ height, the area of our equilateral triangle is $\frac{1}{2}(5\sqrt{3} \times 10)$, or **$25\sqrt{3}$**.

Audacious Arcs and Sensational Sectors

"Arc" is that thing Noah built. "Sector" is an obligatory word in every sci-fi movie.

    Simple enough.

    Or should be.

    Unfortunately, arcs and sectors are also math concepts.

    On a circle, an *arc* is a piece of circumference. A *sector* is a piece of area.

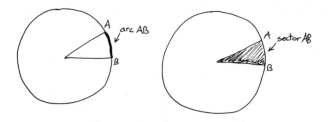

To find the length of an arc or the area of a sector, set up a proportion using the ratio of the central angle to 360°.

Ex.

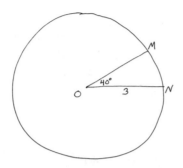

What is the length of minor arc MN in the circle above with center O?

First, let's find out the circumference of the circle. $2\pi r = 2\pi(3)$, or 6π. Set up a proportion:

$$\frac{\text{Arc MN}}{6\pi} = \frac{40}{360°}$$

And solve. $360(\text{Arc MN}) = 240\pi$

Arc MN $= 2\pi/3$

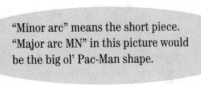

"Minor arc" means the short piece. "Major arc MN" in this picture would be the big ol' Pac-Man shape.

Ex.

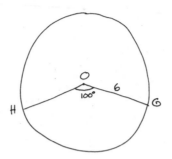

In the circle above with center O and radius 6, what is the area of sector GH?

We'll need to find the area of the circle, which is 36π. Then we'll set up a proportion:

$$\frac{\text{Sector GH}}{36\pi} = \frac{100°}{360°}$$

And solve. $360(\text{Sector GH}) = 3600\pi$

The area of sector GH $= \textbf{10}\boldsymbol{\pi}$

If you're bored, I suggest doodling these problems into monsters. I've done a couple for you; feel free to decorate the others. Send your best to monsters@eliotschrefer.com; Eliot'll use them to replace the drippy current monsters in any future editions.

MUNDANE: ORDINARY

What You'll Never Again Need to Know About the Third Side of a Triangle

Triangles have three sides. If that's news to you, stop reading and go change your diapers. For the rest of us, that always seemed like a fairly unextraordinary concept. To the SAT writers, however, it's a source of endless fascination.

Ex. **If the three sides of a triangle are 4, 10, and x, and x is an integer, what is the difference between the minimum and maximum values of x?**

If you're like most students, your first reaction to this problem will be to make a right triangle with sides of 4 and 10, with x as the hypotenuse. You won't even know why; it'll just feel right. But you'll get $\sqrt{116}$ for x, which does us no good whatsoever.

Oddly and miraculously, this problem has nothing to do with right triangles. Instead, it's an exercise of imagination. Imagine the triangle that had sides of 4 and 10 and the biggest x possible:

x would come close to being 14. It couldn't actually *be* 14, because then you'd have a straight line instead of a triangle. But it could be very close. Since it's an integer, x is the number just less than 14, or 13.

Now imagine a triangle with sides of 4 and 10 and the smallest x possible:

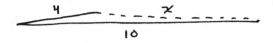

NONCHALANT: COOL

This time x will approach 6. It can't actually *be* 6 or less, because the triangle would close entirely. But it can be close: 7 is the nearest.

So now we have our maximum and minimum x's: 13 and 7. The difference between them is **6**.

You can remember this concept theoretically, or just memorize this:

The third side of a triangle must be less than the sum of the other two sides, and greater than their difference.

Ex. **If Abercrombie is 10 yards from The Gap, and The Gap is 11 yards from Lane Bryant, all of the following are possible values for the number of yards from Abercrombie to Lane Bryant EXCEPT:**

A. 1   D. 21

B. $\sqrt{221}$ E. 22

C. 20

It would be easy to assume that the stores are all in a line, but that's not necessarily true. So they could form a triangle. Given the rule above, we know that the third side has to be more than 1 and less than 21. It could also *be* 1 or 21, if the stores were indeed in a straight line. So the only number that doesn't fit is **E**, 22, which is too much.

Slope's Sequel: Slippery-er Than Ever

Slope seemed all-important for a while there in ninth grade. Every math quiz would ask you to write out the slope formula, or to calculate the slope of some line. And then it stopped being important, like a teen drama in its third season. Slope isn't a prerequisite for more advanced concepts, which means you've probably forgotten about it by now.

Sucker.

SAT geometry loves slope. Can't get enough of it. It's the ultimate SAT question type, actually, since it gets to take a simple concept and warp it into some surprisingly difficult problems. Remember, slope is:

$$\frac{\Delta y}{\Delta x}, \text{ or } \frac{y_2 - y_1}{x_2 - x_1} \quad \text{which means that: } \text{Slope is} \frac{\text{Change in } y}{\text{Change in } x}$$

So the slope of the line crossing points (1, −2) and (3, 6) is

$$\frac{-\text{-}2 - 6}{1 - 3}, \quad \text{or}$$

$$\frac{-8}{-2}, \quad \text{which equals 4.}$$

But of course, the SAT can pervert this otherwise respectable, straightforward concept.

$\mathcal{E}x$. **If line *l* passes through the origin, (5, 2.5), and (3*t* − 6, *t*), what is the value of *t*?**

As in all geometry problems that don't have a predrawn picture, we need to draw one straightaway:

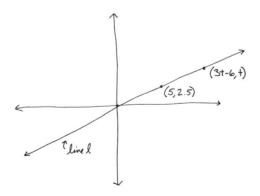

First thing we need to find out is the slope. Since the line passes through (5, 2.5) and (0, 0), we can determine that the slope equals **2.5 − 0/5 − 0**, or ½. Slope is the same everywhere on a line, so we can insert any pair of points and know that their slope must be ½.

So we can pair (3*t*−6, *t*) with any other point, and know that the slope must be ½. Let's choose (0, 0), because it makes the math easier:

$$\frac{t-0}{3t-6-0} = \frac{1}{2}$$

Cross-multiply:

$$2t = 3t - 6$$
$$-t = -6$$
$$t = 6$$

Ex. **Abby stores her paintball guns in a shed whose ceiling rises from 40 feet high at the east wall to 90 feet high at the center, 60 feet away. How high is the ceiling just 3 feet from the wall?**

We weren't given a picture, so it's drawing time:

You'd better not draw anything this detailed on the real thing, or you'll lose tons of time and make me very, very angry. I would be most impressed with your use of perspective, however.

While lovely, this picture has a bit too much detail for us to use it. So instead, let's put the front of the shed in the coordinate plane, with the bottom left corner as (0, 0):

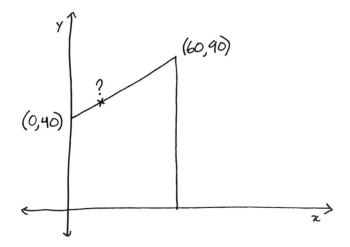

As in the previous problem, once we find the line's slope we can determine the coordinates of any point along the line. And since we have a pair of points, we have enough to determine the slope of the roof:

$$\frac{90-40}{60-0} = \frac{50}{60},$$

Or 5/6.

Since the slope has to be valid for any pair of points on the line, let's find the y value (height) when the x value (distance along the floor) is 3. Our two points will be $(3, y)$ and $(60, 90)$, and the slope between them has to be 5/6.

$$\frac{90-y}{60-3} = \frac{5}{6}$$

Cross-multiply:

$$540 - 6y = 285$$
$$-6y = -255$$
$$y = 42.5$$

Why a More Difficult Test Administration Doesn't Mean Lower Scores

You walk out of the SAT and say, "Yikes! That was so much harder than any practice test I've ever taken! I'm screwed!"

First, you need to lower your voice. You're being a total drama queen.

Second, you're probably just being harder on yourself because it was the real thing, so you're naturally more anxious.

Third, even if the SAT you took was objectively harder than most, that doesn't mean your scores will be any lower. Why? It's a standardized test, which means that your score is the result of a comparison against other test takers taking the test at the same time. So if the average student misses 2.1 more math problems than usual, all the scores will be bumped up to reflect that. So take a chill pill, as my friends from the nineties would say.

The only time you need to listen to those nagging doubts is if the test was especially hard *only for you*. If your friends thought it was easy, but you didn't know ten words, or you only got one paragraph into the essay when time was called, or you had to skip five math questions when you normally answer every one, then you're right to freak out. Sounds like a good case for *cancelling your score*.

A WORD ABOUT CANCELLING SCORES:

Your request to cancel your score must be received by ETS by 11:59 P.M. on the Wednesday following the test date. You can fax the request to them or express mail it, but you can't cancel your scores online.

Faxes get lost, and even express mail can arrive too late, so if you're certain right away that you're going to cancel your score, get a suitable form from the head test proctor and fill it out before you even leave the center. Done. Your test won't be scored, and you won't have that nasty result on your record.

Keep in mind, though, that to cancel any Subject Test scores from one test administration, you have to cancel every test you took that day.

ORTHODOX: CONVENTIONAL

Anxious Areas, Voluminous Volume, and Sneaky Surface Area

These are three separate beasts that have some significant overlap.

Anxious Areas

The area of a square is the square of any side. Okay. Fair enough.

The area of a rectangle is length × width. Sure.

But the area of a trapezoid? Egad.

This one isn't written at the beginning of each

Math section, so you'd better rememorize:

Ex.

Area of a trapezoid = (the average of its bases) × (its height).

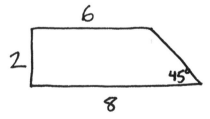

Note: Figure Not To Scale

What is the area of the trapezoid in the figure above?

Our formula asks us to average the bases and multiply by the height, or

$$\frac{8+6}{2} \times 2 = 14$$

The long way around on this problem, by the way, is to drop an altitude and make a special triangle on the right and a rectangle on the left, and come up with their separate areas:

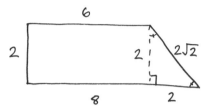

Doable, certainly, but not nearly as easy.

The other kinds of areas you might encounter are the "tile" sorts of problems, in which you are required to fit one area into another:

Ex. **Scarlett O'Hara wants to cover Tara's balcony in tiles that look like the following:**

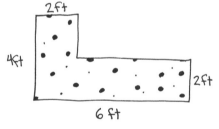

How many tiles will she require to tile the balcony, if its dimensions are 20 yards by 28 yards (1 yard = 3 feet)?

Since we have different units (feet for the tiles, yards for the balcony), *our first duty is to convert ours units.* Easiest will be to convert yards to feet.

That tile's got strep throat. I've seen tiles with strep, and that is one sick tile. I'm sure of it.

20 yards × 3 = 60 feet
28 yards × 3 = 84 feet

So the area of the balcony is 60×84 feet, or 5040 ft^2.

Now, here's when the more conscientious among you will be tempted to determine exactly how these tiles are going to fit into the larger space. *But you don't need to.* This is the SAT, not Tetris, and there are no bonus points for cleverness. In the history of these sorts of problems, exactly how these pieces will fit hasn't been tested. Simply come up with the larger area and divide it by the smaller.

So what's the area of each tile?

Let's split it into smaller units, like this:

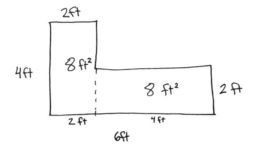

Each tile, therefore, has an area of 16 ft^2. Dividing the larger area by the smaller (5040/16), we find that we'll require **315 tiles.**

The same goes for **volumes**:

Ex. **How many $2 \times 3 \times 7$ ft boxes of Rambo Protein Powder will fit into a $10 \times 15 \times 35$ ft delivery truck?**

Just divide the larger volume (5250) by the smaller (42), and you get **125 boxes** as your answer.

You might also be required to convert a volume to a surface area.

Ex. **If a cube has a volume of 0.729, what is its surface area?**

> **Volume of a cube is s^3. Surface area of a cube is $6s^2$.**

The volume of a cube is, fittingly enough, the cube of any edge, or s^3. Let's solve for the edge of this cube:

$$s^3 = 0.729$$
$$s = \sqrt[3]{0.729}$$
$$s = 0.9$$

The **surface area** of a cube, however, is $6s^2$. (It is, in other words, the area of one face times the number of faces, which we all know from dice gambling—er, watching people gamble on TV— is six.) So the surface area of this cube is $6(0.9)^2$, or **4.86.**

geek!

Fascinating that the surface area is so much greater than the volume, isn't it? That tiny volumes have proportionally greater surface areas explains many of the properties of insects, actually: that because of their smaller dimensions they can have an exoskeleton and not be crushed by its weight, that they can lift so much, that they can walk on the surface of water.

The Witches Who Refuse to Be Defined

PRIME, INTEGER, ZERO, RATIONAL, SETS, AND

FROM/THROUGH/BETWEEN

I couldn't let you finish the Math section without saddling you with a few definitions. The truth is, I knew you'd break out in a rash if I slammed you with anything resembling a math glossary first thing, so I was cowardly and put them in at the end.

That these definitions come at the end doesn't make them any less important; in fact, they're vital.

Prime Numbers: You've probably been taught that a prime number is a number that is only divisible by itself and 1. But that gets sticky, because it begs the question: Is 1 itself prime?

No, it's not. The best definition is that *a prime number has exactly two factors*. Seven is prime, for example, because it has exactly two factors (7 and 1). Ten isn't, because it has four factors . . . one isn't, because it has only one.

The first five prime numbers, therefore, are 2, 3, 5, 7, and 11.

Integer: An integer is any number (positive, negative, or zero) that doesn't have a decimal or fraction (they are "normal numbers"). For example, 5, 1000, −91, and 0 are all integers. 5.5, −⅓, and $\sqrt{2}$ are not.

In SAT terms, an "edge" refers to the line joining two faces.

Zero: The concept of zero is trickier than it seems. A whole book was recently written about theories of zero, actually. What's important here is that you remember a few definitional things:

Zero is an integer.

Zero is neither positive nor negative.

Zero *is* even.

Math problems will commonly ask you to identify a prime number in a set. There are a couple of fakes that we always think of as prime, but they aren't. Learn by my mistake and don't be fooled by these two-faced fake-primes:

39 (3 × 13 = 39),

and

51 (3 × 17 = 51).

Neither of them is prime.

Rational: Any number that can be expressed as a fraction of two integers. If it has a decimal, the decimal must eventually either end or repeat. 2, 0, ⅓, 4.14141414 . . . , and −22/3 are all rational. $\sqrt{2}$ and π are not.

Sets: These have come up recently on the SAT. They never showed up before, and with good reason: Few high school students have been taught them, unless they happen to have taken college logic courses in their spare time. Fortunately, the sets you'll find will be only in their most basic forms.

A **set** is a group of numbers or symbols, each of which is called a "member" or an "element." {2, 5, 10} is the set containing members (or elements) 2, 5, and 10.

The **empty set** is the set without a single value inside: { }. It's different from {0}, which contains the value of zero. The first could represent the results for a final in which no one showed up, for example, and the second would represent the results for a final in which one student turned in a paper that received a zero.

A **union** of two sets is all the members of either set, without duplicates. So the union of sets {*v, w, x, y, z*} and {*a, b, x, y*} would be the set {*a, b, v, w, x, y, z*}. It is represented by the symbol ∪.

The **intersection** of two sets is all the members they have in common. The intersection of the two sets above would be $\{x, y\}$. It is represented by the symbol $\cap$.

Ex.

Tough final!

Given the following sets:
A: {Scarlett, Lindsay, Hilary, Paris, Sienna, Ashley, Mary-Kate}
B: {London, Osaka, Nairobi, Paris, Wales, Corsica, Sienna}
If u equals the number of members of A$\cup$B, and i equals the number of members of A$\cap$B, what is the value of $u-i$?

We're being asked, in other words, for the number of names in the union of A and B minus the number of names in the intersection of A and B.

When we merge them and cross out any duplicates, we get {Scarlett, Lindsay, Hilary, Paris, Sienna, Ashley, Mary-Kate, London, Osaka, Nairobi, ~~Paris~~, Wales, Corsica, ~~Sienna~~}. There are 12 different members, so $u=12$.

The intersection will be only the members they have in common, which is {Paris, Sienna}. So $i=2$.

The value of $u-i$, therefore, is $12-2$, or **10**.

Or,

Ex. **If set P contains all the prime integers, and set E contains all the even integers, what is the intersection of set P and set E?**

We're looking for whatever they have in common, which means we're looking for a number that is both prime and even. There's only one, 2. The answer would be {2}.

PERVASIVE: WIDESPREAD

From/Through/Between: This concept has probably been bugging you for some time. When someone asks, "How many numbers are there from fifteen through twenty-five," it's deceptively simple. Do you include 15, but not 25? Or 25, but not 15? Both? Neither? How's it different from *"between"* 15 and 25?

The words "**from**" and "**through**" mean you include both endpoints. To quickly find the number of numbers, take the

last number – first number + 1.

The number of numbers from 15 through 25 would therefore be $25 - 15 + 1$, or **11.**

"**Between**" means neither endpoint is included. Its formula is:

last number – first number – 1.

The number of numbers between -30 and 10 is $10 - (-30) - 1$, or 39. These lead to a fancy-pants formula that allows you to easily find the sum of a series of consecutive numbers. Simply *take the number of numbers times the average of the endpoints.*

Ex. **What is the sum of all the numbers from 4 through 20?**

(# of #s)(Avg. value)

$(20 - 4 + 1)((4 + 20)/2)$

(17)(12)

204.

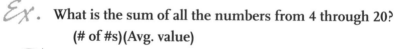

Spotted on the Job, Park Avenue at 87th Street:
Embroidered pillow reading: "If You Want to Be Thinner, Skip Dinner."

Keep Tabs on Your Proctor

Look, your proctor is underpaid, got up way too early on a Saturday, and doesn't know you from Adam. Don't trust that he's got your best interests at heart.

You'd be surprised how often I get students coming to me with stories of crappy proctors. One cut the essay five minutes short. Another forgot to give them a break. Another took away a student's calculator, even though it was permitted on the test.

Depending on how well you know your peers, you're probably not surprised that none of my students did anything about it.

Don't be shy! Don't be a wimp! Or, even if you are normally a wimp, become unwimpy for these very important three hours and forty-five minutes. Don't let your proctor's incompetence interfere with your chance to nail the test. Raise your hand and say that the essay should have been twenty-five minutes, not twenty. Say you're supposed to have a break. Say that you want to see the head proctor, who will confirm that you're allowed to have your calculator.

I took the SAT myself a couple of years ago, just to remember what it was like. The proctor (who was wearing flip-flops and a stained T-shirt and might have smelled like whiskey) forgot his watch, so he asked one of the students to call time on the section. No one said anything until I spoke up and said that it wasn't fair to make a student concentrate on his work and also worry about keeping time. You have to stand up for yourself, guys. Your SAT score is nothing to mess around with.

PETULANT: SULKY

PART IV

WRITING

(Rock-bottom Cheap Tricks
from Your Tutor, with
Commentary from Various
Sassy Students)

Why This Section Is the Easiest of All Three, and Why (Sadly) It Also Matters the Least

This isn't really a writing section; it's about grammar. Sure, there's an essay involved, but it's only one third of the Writing score. The other two thirds are from (this being the SAT and all) multiple choice questions.

Though the essay isn't as important, it gets a lot of press, for a couple of reasons. First, writing an essay is intimidating, and second, it's the only thing on the SAT that your parents feel they know anything about. Figuring out the slope of a line might as well be speaking Swahili to them, but an essay! They've done essays. So if your parents are going to nag you about preparing for the SAT, it's likely going to be about the essay.

But don't listen.

The grammar portions are far more important. And they're very easy to prepare for. In fact, there are only a handful of grammar rules that the SAT loves to test, and they repeat them over and over. So if you can just memorize the rules that we'll lay out in this section, you'll find that the actual test won't be much of a challenge. During test prep, scores on the writing section tend to increase most reliably, and by the most number of points.

Good news, right?

Not really. As most of you know, the SAT used to be out of 1600 points; there were only the Math and Verbal sections, with no writing involved. And though the test might now be out of 2400, old habits die hard. It's a simple reality that your Writing score is going to carry less weight in college admissions than your Math or Critical Reading

POLARIZED: DIVIDED

scores. Substantially less in many cases; a few colleges will ignore it entirely.

You'll notice something as you visit colleges: The smaller the group an admissions officer is talking to, the more secrets she'll divulge. Admissions literature may say that the college considers all three sections of the SAT equally; to a small group, an admissions officer might say that students should concentrate more on the Math and Critical Reading than Writing; meeting one-on-one, the truths start bubbling out. Many colleges simply don't believe that a twenty-five-minute essay can accurately assess a student's writing, and therefore they downplay Writing scores or ignore them entirely. And good for them. A twenty-five-minute essay is unlike anything you've had to do in school, and unlike anything you'll likely have to do in college. Shout out to admissions officers.

So what does that mean for us? We're going to do what it takes to get a good score on the Writing section (because it doesn't take much to raise it), but we're not going to belabor it.

The Real Reasons There's a New SAT

The reasons for a new SAT have as much to do with politics as with education.

In 2001, Richard Atkinson, the president of the University of California system (the largest university system in the country), gave an address questioning the validity of the SAT as an admissions tool, arguing that "I recommended that the university require only standardized tests that assess mastery of specific subject areas rather than undefined notions of aptitude or intelligence. To facilitate this change, I recommended that we no longer require the SAT for students applying to UC." Subsequent analyses of the UC records "concluded that the [Subject Tests] are, in fact, a better predictor of college grades than the SAT."

The only option, he argued, was to push for an SAT based more on actual curricula, or to do away with the test altogether. The College Board, realizing that losing the California system would be the death knell for the SAT, flew out some of its top executives to meet with him. The eventual result was the new SAT, which debuted in 2005 and was touted as a less coachable, more straightforward test. Time has proven, however, that it's just as coachable as it ever was, and the only significant difference is that the Writing section, which used to be a separate (and virtually mandatory) Subject Test, is now rolled into the SAT.

But the biggest impact of this largely cosmetic change has been, of course, that the UC system maintained its SAT requirement, and the SAT remains the most dominant testing force in the country.

POLEMICAL: CONTROVERSIAL

The Essay: Stop Being a Wimp

My students usually harbor little hope for improving on the essay section. How can you learn to write better in just a few weeks? But actually, there's cause for optimism. The Writing section feels difficult because the essay task is so odd—you only have twenty-five minutes to write on an absurdly broad topic, and it's the very first section you'll face on the SAT. You'll sit down at 8:30 A.M., stressed as hell, and immediately face a prompt asking you to write, not about the topic most on your mind (which would be tension, probably, or perhaps the wads of gum dried to the bottom of the desk), but about the "most important quality of a leader" or some similar rot.

But. But. Once you get used to the essay, it's not so bad. Your first attempt to write one will probably be a pathetic and tearful affair. You might write a couple of paragraphs, and the timer will go off in the middle of the third. The reason you won't finish is that you'll instinctively try to write a forty- or forty-five-minute essay, like what you're used to. And you'll only get halfway. But if you can memorize a prefab structure for a twenty-five-minute essay, then all you have to do is tailor it to the topic you've been given. Yeah, it's a cheap trick. But it works wonders.

I can't control how good a writer you are. But that's insignificant: 75 percent of succeeding on the SAT essay is being able to structure such a short paper. Get that out of the way, and you're well on your way to an 800.

Image Is Everything: Three Punctuation Marks No Essay Should Be Without

I recently sat down for lunch with one of my old high school English teachers (I'm a nerd; going to lunch with ex-teachers is what we nerds do). Turns out that, to make extra cash in the summer, she became an SAT essay grader. I paid for her lunch and in return got the inside scoop on what goes on.

Seems that most of your graders are cranky. Your essay is scanned and then e-mailed to a disgruntled teacher somewhere in the country who isn't paid more than $20 an hour, and has about three minutes to allot to your essay. Three minutes ain't much. And don't forget that your graders are scoring hundreds of essays on the *exact same topic*. Talk about mind-numbing. So it's only rational to expect that their brains will start to shut off after a while, and that they just might be scoring you while watching *Jerry Springer*.

They're going to stop reading the essays, and look instead for the *signifiers* of a good essay. So what you need to do is make sure that you include the tell-tale signs of advanced writing, whether or not the essay is actually good.

Crude, but true.

So, what are those signs?

Length. You're only given two pages on which to write your essay, without the option to ask for more. *Fill those pages.* An MIT professor did a study in which he pinned essays on the wall across the room and assigned them scores based solely on how long they looked. And guess what? Those scores were more or less what the essays received. If you have tiny handwriting, make it bigger. If you have big handwriting, keep it big. Don't spend a lot of time planning; don't draft an outline first. Just start writing. I know, this goes against Essay Writing 101, but in this case quantity is better.

Punctuation. A sign of good writing is complex sentence structure. And a sign of complex sentence structure is sophisticated punctuation. You shouldn't inject punctuation you're not comfortable with into your school essays, but on the SAT, it's a gold mine. Here's your foolproof guide:

- *Semicolons.* These join two *independent clauses.* If you have two
❩ consecutive phrases that each have a subject and a verb, then you can put a semicolon in between.

Ex.   *The American Revolution was fought by a ragtag group of malcontents. Only in hindsight have they come to be viewed as heroes.*

These two sentences can easily be joined by a semicolon. Just take out the period and replace it with a ";", then make the following letter lowercase:

The American Revolution was fought by a ragtag group of malcontents; only in hindsight have they come to be viewed as heroes.

Doesn't that look cooler? And since high scores on the essay are based more on image than content, you want an essay that looks cool.

It's okay if semicolons don't come naturally to you. Just look over your essay once you're done, identify two sentences that are closely related, and put a semicolon in between them. The rules of punctuation are flexible enough that you can never be wrong.

( ) *Parentheticals.* Think of these as phrases you'd mutter out of the side of your mouth. Like "Sure, Mom, I'll clean my room (next April!)." Whatever you put in parentheses, your sentence should be able to stand without them; they're like a short, off-topic whisper. What they show is that you're a nuanced thinker, that your mind doesn't operate in only one direction, that you don't take a black-and-white view of the world.

PRECLUDE: PREVENT

Ex. **Say you planned on writing the following:**

Co-ed classrooms provide students with the opportunity to hear as many diverse viewpoints as possible, and to learn to think of their peers as just that—peers.

And you were proud of it, but then you realized once you got halfway through writing the sentence that you were vague about "diverse viewpoints." So you could insert a parenthetical:

Co-ed classrooms provide students with the opportunity to hear as many diverse viewpoints as possible (being exposed only to supportive thoughts about the nineteenth amendment is less helpful than hearing one's views countered), and to learn to think of their peers as just that—peers.

See what parentheses do? They provide non-crucial information that proves you're thinking through the topic.

────── *Dash.* Think of these as semicolons, redux. Use them the same way—they join two independent clauses.

Ex. **Uh, I just wrote one. Take a look.**

Originality. Only worry about the uniqueness of your viewpoint if you're gunning for a top score on the essay. You'll have two graders, each giving you a score of 1–6 each (for a total score of 2 to 12 points). You can get a 4 or even a 5 from your graders if you write a bland and unambitious essay (as long as it's otherwise well written, of course). But to get a 6, you can't write about something your grader has already read a dozen times. So try to imagine what the typical student will say, and claim something radically different, even the opposite. Just don't go offensive and start praising Hitler.

SAMPLE PROMPT:	What is the greatest invention of the twentieth century?
TYPICAL RESPONSE:	*E-mail/Internet, because it connects us more than ever.*
BETTER RESPONSE:	*The telegraph, because it was the first form of instantaneous, long-distance communication.*
SAMPLE PROMPT:	Should censorship of music lyrics be permitted?
TYPICAL RESPONSE:	*No, because freedom of speech is important.*
BETTER RESPONSE:	*Yes, especially in cases of slander or individuals being named in lyrics against their will.*

You see what we're doing here? We're imagining the average response and giving something different, even if it's not our natural reaction. Your first reaction to this last prompt might have been "No, because rap is awesome." But if you're going for a top score, try to defeat that urge and come up with something truly unusual.

Or, you can give a typical response but use unusual examples to prove it, as follows.

Ex. *What is the most important quality in a leader?*

You decide to go with "perseverance." You might be tempted to write about the first leaders you think of—say, George Washington and Winston Churchill. But those are typical. Say you've recently written a paper on Egypt. Then use an Egyptian president. Or use someone who wasn't the leader of a country—a scientific leader like Louis Pasteur. Or even start off by defining a leader not as someone who actively directs but rather leads by providing a positive example, like George Eliot or some obscure saint.

Surprise your grader; make an English teacher's day.

The Cheapest Trick of Them All: Prewriting Your Essay

I've said I want your essay to be as long as possible, but you're only given twenty-five minutes to write it. So how can you make it long? Simple: prewrite. If you go in unprepared, you're going to flounder. But if you go in with a set, memorized structure, then all you have to do is tailor it to the question at hand.

Your prompt will give you a short quote, then direct you further, like this:

Think carefully about the issue presented in the following excerpt and the assignment below.

Situations can worsen invisibly, with such a slow deterioration that the fact that we are dissatisfied becomes imperceptible until a crisis is reached. Other times, quality of life can drop in a moment, and situations immediately go from good to bad. Of the two, the first is the more dangerous, resulting in people who realize they are bored or unhappy with their lives long after they have lost the willpower to do anything about it.

ASSIGNMENT:
Are we better off having bad events happen in a sudden way or slowly progress? Plan and arrive at an essay in which you develop your point of view on this issue. Support your argument with reasoning and examples taken from your reading, studies, experience, or observations.

what a downer!

If you're a slow reader, or easily get muddled, *you can always skip the quotation.* All you'll need in order to properly answer the question will be found in the prompt itself. We can spend our time

PROVINCIAL: UNSOPHISTICATED

reading the depressing quotation (sorry about that; it was raining while I wrote it), or we can skip to the prompt.

Basically, it's asking us if we'd prefer to get bad news in a rush, or slowly ease into it. That's all we need to know.

You'll notice the assignment prompts us to use examples from our "reading, studies, experience, or observations." Unless you're in, say, the top 10 percent of writers, go for reading or studies. Personal experience doesn't make for a high-scoring essay, unless it's pulled off exceptionally well.

Imagine that your essay is your twenty-five-minute chance to sneak a kiss from a textbook author (either a thrilling or nauseating prospect, depending on your tastes). You want to come off as interesting, balanced, and intellectual. You can see how writing about the time you lost your stuffed bear won't accomplish this as well as discussing *Anna Karenina*.

So, right now, come up with a list of three books or plays (of the sort you would read in English class), three historical events, and two scientists or discoveries that you'll feel comfortable with. Beside each one write a few salient facts. You'll be surprised how much better you'll feel with this list in your back pocket on test day (leave it there: if you pull your list out during the test, the proctor will eat you). When we get nervous, abstract thinking is one of the first faculties to go, and you'll be convincing yourself that you don't know anything you could possibly write about. But if you've memorized a list of this length, you'll have examples ready for just about any prompt they can throw at you.

If you're stuck making your list, if you can't remember any of the books you read in English, and you always skipped history to get to lunch early, make a few notes on the following topics, each of which is interesting and broad enough to be applied to just about any essay question. Broadly speaking, SAT prompts tend to be of the "success versus failure" variety, so think of these topics in terms of what it takes to do well at something or generally kick butt:

Science

Charles Darwin: Took a long time to make sure his research was immaculate; postulated that organisms best fit to survive live to reproduce, which leads to gradual improvement in the population. (*On the Origin of Species*, 1859)

Vaccination: In 1796, British country doctor Edward Jenner exposed people to cowpox and thereby inoculated them against the far more dangerous smallpox. Exposure to a minor illness prevents a greater one. The term "vaccination" comes from the Latin *vacca*, or cow.

Literature

The Awakening: Novel written by Kate Chopin, published in 1899. An early feminist work in which a well-to-do young wife struggles to express ambitions that are limited by social and sexual constraints.

The Great Gatsby: Novel written by F. Scott Fitzgerald, published in 1925. Ultimate story of an outsider setting a goal (to be wealthy) and achieving it, though the results aren't all that he might have wanted.

Macbeth: Play written by William Shakespeare, first produced in 1605–6. The classic tale of ambition and its effects on morality, character, and loved ones. Super bloody.

History

15th Amendment/Civil Rights Movement: Knowing the primary leaders and dates of the Civil Rights Movement will be a great help, since you can use them for just about any question about leadership or inspiration. Similar goes for the fight to constitutionally give blacks the vote.

Elizabeth Cady Stanton: Early feminist, whose "Declaration of Sentiments" was the key document of the landmark Seneca Falls women's rights convention, which was the first major push toward women's rights and women's suffrage.

Mohandas Gandhi: A key political and spiritual leader of India whose philosophy of nonviolence helped lead the country to freedom from British rule in 1946.

A Prefab Essay Outline for You to Memorize, to the Chagrin of Every English Teacher You've Ever Had

Introduction

a. SENTENCE 1: *Give your broad response to the topic.*

Be careful not just to restate the question. If you're asked to "give the most important quality of a leader," don't write, "The most important quality in a leader is perseverence." Instead, write, "Of all the traits a leader might possess, the most essential is perseverence."

b. SENTENCE 2: *Mention an abstract, nonspecific case.*

You're discussing the issue theoretically, but not actually getting into your body paragraph examples yet. You could write, "A man or woman who faces difficulties and overcomes them is a true leader." Or better: "Any person can come up with a way to get past an obstacle; to keep others moving forward despite being thwarted is a far more admirable trait."

c. SENTENCE 3: *Give the reason WHY this statement is true.*

Now comes your most important sentence, and your essay hinges on it. You have to scrape as far as you can into your profound side and come up with a deep statement about *why* sentence 2 was true. "Setbacks bring out a person's insecurities—a leader is someone who can face those insecurities and still feel himself qualified to lead others," or "Leaders not only present ideas but model behavior for the rest of us to follow, and nothing is more comforting than a leader whom we're convinced we can always rely on," or "We look to leaders as children look to parents; we'll accept their flaws as long as we're certain they are unconditionally committed to us."

d. SENTENCE 4: *Introduce two examples.*

You can breathe a sigh of relief at this point, because now your essay's on autopilot. All you have to do now is name your two examples. "Two leaders who tenaciously clung to their goals are Theodore Roosevelt and Jean Valjean of Victor Hugo's *Les Misérables*." Or "We can find examples of this truth in the cases of Theodore Roosevelt and Victor Hugo's *Les Misérables*."

2 First Body Paragraph

a. SENTENCE 1: *Topic sentence.*

Here's where it starts to get easy. You've already done the major intellectual work for the essay in the introduction; now you just have to follow through. Your topic sentence brings up your first example. If it's literary, be sure to name the author and get the genre right (if it's by Shakespeare, it's not a novel).

b. SENTENCES 2–4/5: *Discuss concretely.*

Don't feel that you have to constantly prove your point with every sentence—that's when essays start to sound repetitive. Instead, just let yourself depict, in straightforward, nontheoretical language, what's going on in your example.

c. LAST SENTENCE: *Tie back into thesis.*

Now's when you reiterate how the example ties into your main point.

3 Second Body Paragraph

Repeat steps a, b, and c. Except now you're discussing a different example, of course.

4 Conclusion

You could find that once you get to your conclusion you only have two or three minutes left. Which is fine. In a four-paragraph essay, you don't need a massive conclusion. It can be as short as two sentences (though three would be better). The most important thing is that you have one.

a. SENTENCE 1: *Restate your thesis.*

Be careful not to have it sound exactly like the sentence you used in the introduction. Vary your language and syntax.

QUIXOTIC: IDEALISTIC

b. SENTENCE(S) 2–3: *Conclude.*

Finding a conclusion statement can be hard. You have three options:

   i. End with the sentence: "We are continually reminded, therefore, of the significance of being human." Works every time. (I'm joking. Sorta.)

   ii. Glance over your essay. Realize there's something you forgot to say? Work it into the conclusion.

   iii. Refer to the future. If you're writing about the most important quality of a leader, for example, you could close by saying, "If, in coming years, our political leaders persevere as much as Theodore Roosevelt and Jean Valjean did, then we can count on a steadily progressing world community."

Note: These are all cheesy ways to conclude. Which isn't to say they won't give you a high score. But if, while writing your essay, a more natural means of concluding presents itself, by all means do that instead. It'll make your English teachers prouder.

. . . English teachers more proud? Hmm . . . good thing the grammar section's coming up.

Occurred on the Job, 75th Street at 2nd Avenue:

Tutor brought in with express purpose to make thirteen-year-old basketball-star son "more sensitive." As son remained thirteen and male, tutor failed in this goal.

How the Essay Should Break Down
("Break Down" as in Blueprint,
not "Breakdown" as in Whimpering)

Begin your essay on this page. If you need more space, continue on the next page.

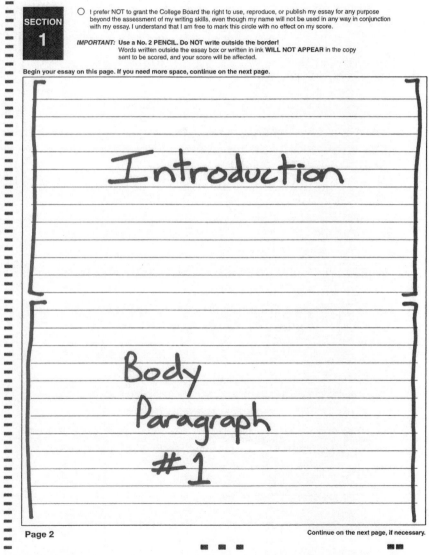

Continue on the next page, if necessary.

RANCOR: RESENTMENT

174

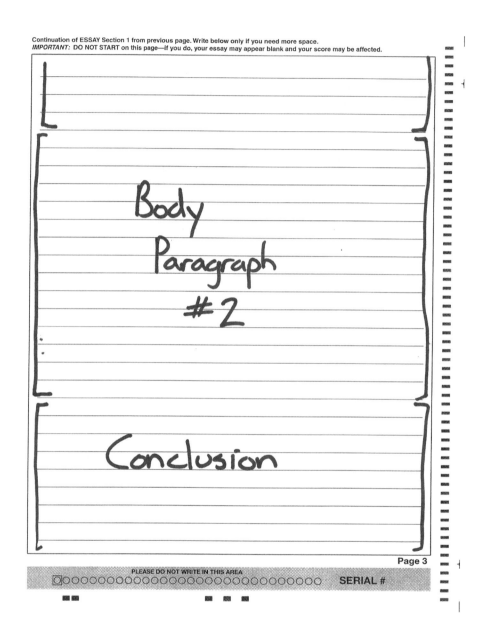

Body

Paragraph

#2

Conclusion

SERIAL #

RECLUSE: LONER

A Real Essay Written by Your Trusty Tutor in Twenty-five Minutes (Timed and Annotated by Students Holding Stopwatches)

Okay, guys. I'm ready. I had my fellow tutor friend write the question, I've got the paper in front of me, and only twenty-five minutes to write the essay. Yipes.

Here's what I'm going to remind myself before I start:

I can cut myself slack if the intro paragraph goes slowly. The introduction is when I have to do all the intellectual work of the essay, after all. By the time my grader's finished the intro, she'll probably have a good idea of what my score will be, so that paragraph's make or break. If it takes ten or fifteen minutes for me to finish just the intro, that's okay. I'll race through the remaining paragraphs.

Timer ready?

Think carefully about the issue presented in the following excerpt and the assignment below.

Some claim that with hard work anyone can achieve success. Others say that effort and determination will only get a person so far, that without the talent and advantages granted at birth, some goals will forever be out of reach.

ASSIGNMENT:
Which is more important for success, hard work or innate gifts? Plan and arrive at an essay in which you develop your point of view on this issue. Support your argument with reasoning and examples taken from your reading, studies, experience, or observations.

SECTION 1

IMPORTANT: Use a No. 2 PENCIL. Do NOT write outside the border!
Words written outside the essay box or written in ink **WILL NOT APPEAR** in the copy sent to be scored, and your score will be affected.

Begin your essay on this page. If you need more space, continue on the next page.

It's hard to distinguish what we're working towards from who we are — our natural tendencies form the kernel our work ethic is founded on. A man might fool himself into thinking his willpower can control his future, but that very willpower is the product of experiences acting on his personality from birth. Because our desire to work hard stems from a sense of our potential that hinges on our innate gifts having been recognized, innate gifts are ultimately essential to self-improvement. But examples such as Charles Darwin and Lucy Honeychurch in E.M. Forster's A Room With a View prove that the nature of these gifts can be broad indeed.

   In retrospect we might think of Darwin as a classic scientific success story, but his real journey towards his breakthroughs was convoluted! As a naturalist aboard the HMS Beagle in the 1830s, Darwin came across many new and outlandish creatures. That he worked hard to catalogue them is undeniable, but his real success was to remain patient & suspend judgment for as long as possible. Possessed of a cautious nature, Darwin sat with his observations before leaping to any conclusions. As a result, he didn't publish his Origin of Species until a full 25

Page 2   Continue on the next page, if necessary.

REMUNERATION: PAYMENT

You sound like you're *really* fun at parties.

Good first sentence—goes straight into the heart of the subject. But you shouldn't have ended a sentence with a preposition.

Um . . . I'd like to point out that that's not Darwin's full title. It's actually *On the Origin of Species by Means of Natural Selection, or the Preservation of Favoured Races in the Struggle for Life.*

Continuation of ESSAY Section 1 from previous page. Write below only if you need more space.
IMPORTANT: DO NOT START on this page—if you do, your essay may appear blank and your score may be affected.

years later. But it was such a meticulously researched, thought-out work that it gave his theory of natural selection the burst of critical momentum it needed to secure Darwin a prominent place in the history of science.

Lucy Honeychurch, the protagonist of Forster's *A Room With a View*, isn't initially presented as an extraordinary figure; she's just a conventional British girl travelling to Italy in the early 20th century. She feels vaguely dissatisfied with her life, but doesn't know how to move towards a greater happiness. No amount of introspection helps, until she finally opens herself up to the prospect of love—from a man who isn't her fiancé. Her desires bubble out despite her efforts to repress them. Since Forster presents Lucy's breaking of her engagement as the key to her eventual happiness, we discover that her irrepressible natural instincts led her to personal success despite her hard work to the contrary.

It's tempting to set up an arbitrary distinction between hard work and natural tendencies, while in truth the two inform each other. Who we are can either speed along our hard work to succeed, or open up possibilities for happiness that might be far different from what we're striving for. This interconnectedness is hardly surprising—who we are says everything about what we work towards.

Page 3

REPUDIATE: DENY

Yay, semicolon!

12/12. But choking on a butcher knife would have been more fun.

Eh. 8 out of 12.

Grammar

The grammar multiple choice questions come in three varieties:

Improving Sentences

These questions require you to analyze the underlined part of a question and determine which answer choice is the best version. Don't bother reading choice A; it's always just a repeat of the sentence as written.

Ah, we finally come to it! I ask you to prepare, folks, for the sweetest sensation on all this earth: half an hour of grammar rules.

Ex. Biff told his date all about his computer game but she was <u>annoyed tuning out all his prattling about enraged griffons, sorcerous lizardmen, and dual level ranger-clerics</u>.

- a. annoyed tuning out all his prattling about enraged griffons, sorcerous lizardmen, and dual level ranger-clerics.
- b. annoyed, tuning out all his prattling about enraged griffons, sorcerous lizardmen, and dual level ranger-clerics.
- c. annoyed; thereby she tuned out all his prattling about enraged griffons, sorcerous lizardmen, and dual level ranger-clerics.
- d. annoyed and in being so tuned out all his prattling about enraged griffons, sorcerous lizardmen, and dual level ranger-clerics.

e. **annoyed because she was not able to tune out all his prattling about enraged griffons, sorcerous lizardmen, and dual level ranger-clerics.**

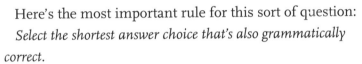

Okay, granted the Dungeons and Dragons vocab might be its own turnoff, but when you look at the sentence, does one answer choice stick out as better? **B**, perhaps?

Choice A is correct about 20 percent of the time. That is, the sentence given to you is already right about one in five times.

Here's the most important rule for this sort of question: *Select the shortest answer choice that's also grammatically correct.*

These questions test your knowledge of grammar and also your sense of style (and no, your Diesel jeans will get you nowhere). Luckily, the SAT writers have an incredibly basic definition of writing style: They just want you to use the fewest words you can.

I once had a student who, as far as I could tell, hadn't ever read anything beyond his friends' tattoos. After a few weeks of futile effort at teaching him grammar rules

You generally want to avoid going for answer choices that include "being" or "the fact that"—both phrases are signs of wordiness.

("Parentheses? WTF are those?"), I just had him select the shortest answer choice on every question of this type. And he was right half the time. Take a look at the example above—B also just happens to be one of the shortest two choices.

Identifying Sentence Errors

Most students find these harder. You're given a (potentially) flawed sentence, and then have to pinpoint what's wrong with it. Which is hard, because often the sentences are so awkward that more than one answer seems likely.

> *Ex.* **Biff continued <u>to try</u> to impress his date by recounting his**
>   _A
> <u>**various**</u> **adventures with the Biker Gang that raised him; but despite**
>   _B
> **his tales of flaming bike jumps and souped-up Harleys, she <u>was</u>**
>   _C
> **unimpressed by <u>their civilization. No error</u>**
>   _D   _E

Hmm. A lot of things can seem wrong with this sentence (Biff continued to try to impress a date who was incapable of respecting his individuality, first off). This question type can be hard for even the most advanced student, because this sentence is not written the same way that you would have written it. So all sorts of things can seem iffy. In order to avoid jumping too quickly, use this rule of thumb:

Only choose A through D if you can make a mental correction. *If you can't think of an alternative that would make the sentence better, then choose E instead.*

Choices A through C above might not feel great, but it's hard to imagine a correction that would make them better. "Trying" instead of "to try"? Maybe. But it's not like "to try" is *wrong*.

Why Rich Kids Are Apparently Slower (Gaming the Extended Time Learning Disabilities System)

Learning disabilities are ascribed to a number of causes—from dyslexia to ADHD to physical handicaps—but can be reduced to the same concept: that speed of learning is an issue quite unrelated to intelligence, and that the student who takes twice as long to grasp a reading passage won't necessarily emerge with any less profound an understanding. Until 2003, students who took the SAT under nonstandard conditions would have their scores flagged. As the test makers themselves officially report, extra time "may overcompensate for some students, permitting them to respond more leisurely and result in overpredictions of college performance," so word in the test-prep community was that college admissions committees would therefore unofficially deduct around seventy points from scores so marked. But in 1999, when the Educational Testing Service was sued by a disabled student who contended that flagging his extra time was unfair, ETS settled out of court and agreed not to mark abnormal test administrations any longer. Once that stigma was removed, getting extra time became an irrefutably favorable proposition—150 percent or even 200 percent of the time other students receive, and colleges will never know. On the new SAT, the benefits are even more exaggerated. Imagine an essay written in twenty-five minutes being directly compared to one written in fifty. And that doesn't factor in even more unusual accommodations—students permitted to write the essay on a keyboard, taking the test in a private chamber for social anxiety disorder, or dictating responses to a scribe.

Little wonder, then, that ambitious families maximize every opportunity to obtain extra time. ETS doesn't release statistics on regional variations in special accommodations, but after years working in test prep under an umbrella group that employs a hundred other tutors to do the same, I found the portion of Manhattan students receiving extra time on the SAT to come up near 40 percent—nationwide, it's under 2 percent. It's not that there's something funny in the water on Park Avenue. The discrepancy stems from a competitive island atmosphere, to be sure, but it is also undeniable that pursuing extra time accommodations requires money—a lot of it. The process must be begun years in advance of the SAT, and involves extensive psychological evaluations and the backing of a school that has sufficient resources to champion the student to ETS. The process is institutionalized in Manhattan private schools, but requires tremendous initiative and time/money elsewhere. The primary criterion for having extra time granted for the SAT is that you've already been receiving it in school. If you suspect you need extra time, talk to your parents and guidance counselor as soon as possible.

SANGUINE: CHEERFUL

Similarly, you might want to cut out the word "various," since it feels unnecessary. *But you can't cut out an answer blank entirely; you can only modify it.*

What's the correct answer above? **D.** D's our guy because of one of the most overlooked rules in the grammar book, the collective noun. "Gang" is singular, not plural. (Think about it: Would you say "the gang is large" or "the gang are large"? *Is.* Which means it's singular.) And since "gang" is singular, you'd have to say "*its* civilization," not "*their* civilization." This rule is very important, and you'll be hearing it again soon.

Paragraph Improvement

These questions are the easiest of the bunch. You'll get a pretend student essay, often hilariously poorly written, and you'll be asked how to improve it.

Using the strategies I've discussed above and the grammar rules we're about to go into, you should be able to sail through these. One specific word of advice about them, however:

These essays tend to be overwritten, therefore *if a question gives you the option to "omit" or "delete" a sentence or group of words, there's a better than even chance that that's what you should do.*

Ex. (1) Some people say that Oreos are the best cookie. (2) But they are wrong. (3) Being superfine, the better cookie is the Vienna Finger. (4) Even people who don't know the first thing about cookies they are agreeing about it. (5) The Vienna Finger's qualities are numerous: it is tasty, it is inexpensive, and even your parents will have been eating them for as long as they will remember. (6) Not just cookies are good, but also cakes. (7) But I love this for one reason, and one reason solely: it is always crunchy, and the cream filling is always delicious.

SCATHING: HARSH

1. In context, which of the following revisions is necessary in sentence 4 (reproduced below)?

   Even people who don't know the first thing about cookies they are agreeing about it.

   a. Delete "first"

   b. Change "don't" to "didn't"

   c. Change "know" to "understand"

   d. Insert "the making of" before "cookies."

   e. Change "they are agreeing about it" to "agree."

2. What should be done with sentence 6 (reproduced below)?

   Not just cookies are good, but also cakes.

   a. Leave it as it is.

   b. Delete it.

   c. Insert "Therefore" at the beginning.

   d. Rephrase the sentence and begin with "This may sound extraneous, but."

   e. Add "no matter what people say" to the end.

3. In context, which of the following most logically replaces "this" in sentence 7 (reproduced below)?

   But I love this for one reason, and one reason solely: it is always crunchy, and the cream filling is always delicious.

   a. Vienna Fingers

   b. this cake of mine

   c. this argument

   d. the Vienna Finger

   e. cookies in general

Answers:

1 E—it makes the writing more concise.

2 B—deleting is always a good idea.

3 D—the sentence refers to Vienna Fingers, but only in the singular ("*it is always crunchy*").

SCRUPULOUS: MORAL

Three Tough Question Types You Will Definitely Face

Some of the grammar rules the SAT tests are so common that I'm putting them in their own section. These are the most essential rules for grammar, the concepts you'll see at least once a test. If you learn nothing else, learn these.

*1*INCORRECT: *The audience of wild dogs, Cheshire cats, and schoolchildren are listening politely to the emperor's announcement.*

Ask yourself: What's the subject? Any time you see an "of" in a sentence, start a bracket and end it whenever you get to the verb, like this:

The audience [of wild dogs, Cheshire cats, and schoolchildren] are listening politely to the emperor's announcement.

Then ignore the bracket. *The audience . . . are listening politely?* No way. *The audience is listening politely.*

CORRECT: *The audience of wild dogs, Cheshire cats, and schoolchildren is listening politely to the emperor's announcement.*

I remember this rule from the last page.

Rule 1. Bracket and ignore all clauses beginning with "of."

2. Test all verbs—singular subjects need singular verbs, and plural subjects need plural verbs.

*2*INCORRECT: *Its superior storage capacity and sleek look makes the Louis Vuitton bag an obvious choice for any fashionista's collection.*

This one's a close relative of the last rule. You've got to make sure that, if you name two things and they both are doing an action, the verb is in its plural form.

CORRECT: *Its superior storage capacity and sleek look* ***make*** *the Louis Vuitton bag an obvious choice for any fashionista's collection.*

Thanks for the $50,000 kickback, Louis!

Rule: If you have two subjects, then your verb must be plural.

INCORRECT: *If a member of the lacrosse team wants to compete in Saturday's tournament, they should express their intention by saying "yip, yip, yip!"*

Do not use "they" just because you don't know the gender of someone. You can only use "they" for plurals. If you don't know the gender, pick "he," "she," or "he/she." (Personally, I hate "he/she" and just choose one of the two pronouns, but that's a personal choice, like flossing only at night or refusing to wear man-sandals.)

CORRECT: *If a member of the lacrosse team wants to compete in Saturday's tournament,* ***she*** *should express* ***her*** *intention by saying "yip, yip, yip!"*

Rule: Only use "they" for plurals; even if you're unsure of gender you still have to use a "he" or a "she."

SERENE: TRANQUIL

Eleven Grammar Rules Accompanied by Whimsical Example Sentences,
OR Your Tutor Discovers the Tiny Subset of English Grammar That Is the SAT's Secret Lover

NOTE: You won't have to literally rewrite sentences on your SAT; it's just how I'm presenting the rules that will be tested via the question types in the last section. For a reminder about question types, see page 180.

The Writing multiple choice section of the SAT is supposed to test your knowledge of English grammar, but what it actually tests is a small subset of rules over and over. What follows are the eleven grammar rules the SAT loves to test, listed in order of frequency, each accompanied by an example sentence.

INCORRECT: *Known for its stunning views and rugged landscape, thousands of tourists visit the cove each year.*

Ask yourself: What's "known for its stunning views and rugged landscape"? Not "thousands of tourists," that's for sure! It's the cove, which means the cove has to come after the comma.
CORRECT: *Known for its stunning views and rugged landscape, the cove is visited by thousands of tourists each year.*

Rule: If a sentence starts with a descriptive phrase, whatever follows the comma must be what is being described.

Beware especially of collective nouns, which seem plural but are actually singular:

Audience	Office
Group	Association
Assembly	Crew
Company	

SOLICIT: ASK

2 INCORRECT: *The novels of Jane Austen are more widely read than Charlotte and Emily Brontë combined.*

Ask yourself: What are we really comparing here? Novels and people, or novels and novels? Novels and novels, of course!

CORRECT: *The novels of Jane Austen are more widely read than **those of** Charlotte and Emily Brontë combined.*

> **Rule:** In any sentence containing the word "than," test that the comparison is logical.

3 INCORRECT: *In the middle of the party Zach noticed that he forgot to put pants on.*

We have two actions going on here—Zach's noticing his pantless condition, and his earlier forgetting to put pants on. They occur at different times, but in this sentence they're written in the same tense—tsk, tsk.

CORRECT: *In the middle of the party Zach noticed that he **had forgotten** to put pants on.*

> **Rule:** If two actions are occuring at different times, they need different tenses.

Have you been reading this book straight through, without a break? Go eat a biscuit.

*4*INCORRECT: *I'm always embarrassed when I see how slow my model sailboat goes.*

Be careful about adjectives and adverbs. In the majority of cases, adverbs end in -ly, and they're the words to use if you're describing an action. The model sailboat may be *slow,* but it moves *slowly.*

CORRECT: *I'm always embarrassed when I see how slowly my model sailboat goes.*

> **Rule:** Be careful to use adverbs (not adjectives) to describe actions or adjectives.

*5*INCORRECT: *With its yellow color, salty taste, as well as chemical odor, Red Bull is one of the nastiest culinary developments of recent years.*

When you're listing items, make sure that they're set up identically. You don't want to start with two things that are set up the same ("yellow color, salty taste") and then mess it all up with a phrase like "as well as."

CORRECT: *With its yellow color, salty taste, and chemical odor, Red Bull is one of the nastiest culinary developments of recent years.*

> **Rule:** Use "and" for simple lists.

BEWARE OF THE FOLLOWING TRICKY CONJUGATIONS:

PRESENT	PAST	DISTANT PAST
I swim	I swam	I had swum
I sneak	I sneaked	I had sneaked (not snuck)
I sing	I sang	I had sung
I lie (down)	I lay (down)	I had lain (down)
I lay (something down)	I laid (something down)	I had laid (something down)
I rise	I rose	I had risen

*6*INCORRECT: *Even though we were all brought up to think that Tyrannosaurus Rexes were the deadliest dinosaurs, kids today are learning that it is, at best, fourth on the list of big prehistoric killers.*

Here, the Tyrannosaurus starts out plural ("were"), and then becomes singular ("it"). Can't do that.
CORRECT: *Even though we were all brought up to think that Tyrannosaurus Rexes were the deadliest dinosaurs, kids today are learning that **they are**, at best, fourth on the list of big prehistoric killers.*

> **Rule:** Something that starts out singular or plural can't switch to the opposite.

*7*INCORRECT: *I paused the music video at the part where the kids get thrown in the pool.*

"Where" is a tricky word. In spoken English, we'll frequently use it instead of a variety of more pretentious-sounding phrases, like "in which" or "to which." But you shouldn't use it in formal writing (or on the SAT) unless you're referring to a literal, physical place.
CORRECT: *I paused the music video at the part **in which** the kids get thrown in the pool.*

> **Rule:** Only use "where" to refer to physical places; only use "when" to describe times.

SUBSTANTIATE: VALIDATE

8 INCORRECT: *The birthday card, which was carefully signed by Randy's family and I, failed to say "Happy Birthday" anywhere on it.*

Whoops. Hope Randy's laid back.

Ah, the "I" versus "me" issue. Your parents probably did you a disservice here. By indiscriminately correcting "me" to "I" while we were growing up, some of our parents inadvertently taught us that "I" just sounds more polite than "me." But often it's not better. "I" is the subject form, which you use for something that's doing an action. "Me" is the object form, which you use for something that's receiving the action.

Whenever you have a pronoun that comes after a preposition (of, from, by, because), it has to be the object form (me, him, whom, us, them), not the subject form (I, he, who, we, they).

CORRECT: *The birthday card, which was carefully signed by Randy's family and **me**, failed to say "Happy Birthday" anywhere on it.*

Rule: When unsure of pronouns, try reading the sentence without the surrounding proper nouns.

Best way to tell which pronoun to use?
Try reading the sentence without the proper nouns.
Would you say "signed by I" or "signed by me"?
Me. Bingo.

SULLEN: SULKY

*9*INCORRECT: *The principal and vice principal listened carefully to the teachers' complaints, and the teachers listened to the officials' rebuttals, but in the end they decided the other side was a bunch of whiners.*

Whenever you see a pronoun in a sentence, you must be able to point to a specific noun it refers to. Here, we're just not sure whom "they" references.

CORRECT: *The principal and vice principal listened carefully to the teachers' complaints, and the teachers listened to the officials' rebuttals, but in the end **the officials** decided the other side was a bunch of whiners.*

Rule: Avoid ambiguous pronouns.

*10*INCORRECT: *Eliza is the craziest of the twins.*

If you're comparing two things, you have to use an "-er" word; "-est" words are reserved for three or more. ("My mother is the kinder of my parents." "He is the kindest kid in my class.") Similarly, use "more" or "less" for two, and "most" or "least" for three or more. ("Fido is the more aggressive of the two dogs, and Ruffles is the least aggressive kitten in his whole litter.")

CORRECT: *Eliza is the **crazier** of the twins.*

Rule: "-er" is used for comparing two things; "-est" is for three or more.

11 INCORRECT: *Manhattan has plenty of tall buildings but not many of its trees are tall.*

Parallelism is a popular concept on the Writing section. It says that you should have similar clauses set up identically. If this sentence were constructed correctly, the buildings and trees would be set up similarly, with an adverb and an adjective coming right before each one. CORRECT: *Manhattan has plenty of tall buildings **but few tall trees**.*

That's all your tutor has to say about grammar, friends. I know these rules are so numbing your dentist could inject them into your gums before drilling (ba-*dum*-dum), but knowing them backward and forward is the surest way to earn yourself a bunch of points. And you'll be helping yourself sound smarter for the rest of your life, which has to pay off eventually. You'll be hitting on an English major someday and thinking, "Thank you, Eliot, now I get why you put me through that." Don't forget to look over the essay section, too, of course, but remember: Grammar is where it's at.

Congratulations: You made it through all three sections! It would seem our time together is drawing to a close. But wait . . . what's this . . .

TACTILE: RELATING TO TOUCH

PART V

BEATING THE FINAL BOSS

(What to Do with Everything You've Learned, Including a Practice Drill and Applications Advice)

Having managed to avoid falling asleep in the Critical Reading section, tearing up the Math section, and wiping your bum with the Grammar rules, you thought yourself pretty well prepared for your SAT.

But you're wrong.

What you've done is the equivalent of getting through every level of a video game, learning how to demolish the various peons that appear on every level, and then advancing unprepared to the final boss level.

We'll get you through the actual test day.

And hell, it's not just about the SAT—let's get you into college to boot.

Love the massive amounts of parallelism in that first sentence!

Where to Practice Everything You've Learned Herein

Back in the "You Come Up with a Preparation Plan" section I told you the best way to prepare after reading this book: lots of practice tests. So get off your duff and download your first one for free from collegeboard.org.

Once you've finished, get your hands on the official SAT book, the one with the real practice tests. Take all of those, one each week until the test.

Kaplan (kaplan.com; sign up online) offers one free practice test for anyone who wants to come in on a Saturday morning. I highly recommend it—they'll score your test (including the essay) on the spot, and you'll have a taste of what it feels like to take an exam when you aren't in your pajamas.

I suggest all of this preparation knowing full well that a whole bunch of you will do none of it.

For you slackers (and for the more diligent among you as well) I've

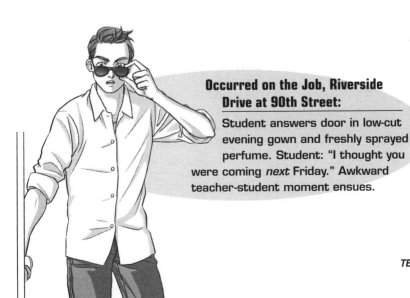

Occurred on the Job, Riverside Drive at 90th Street:

Student answers door in low-cut evening gown and freshly sprayed perfume. Student: "I thought you were coming *next* Friday." Awkward teacher-student moment ensues.

TEDIUM: BORINGNESS

written the following practice drill. It's not meant to feel like taking a real SAT. But it's a set of questions that will help you assess how much you've gotten out of this book, and identify which sections you need to revisit. As a whole, these problems are harder than the average SAT section. But they'll cover the most essential rules, with page numbers beside their answers if you get confused.

TEMPERATE: MODERATE

SAT Drill

Math

1. If, of the 30 contestants on a Fox show, 21 are shameless thrill seekers and 14 have talent, at least how many are talented and shameless thrill seekers?

2. If the length of minor arc AB is 7.5π, what is the area of sector AB?

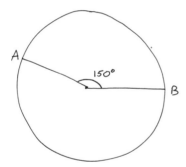

3. If a day of fan mail for *America's Premier Shoe Salesman* can fill a cubic box with an edge of 3 feet, how many days of mail will fill a 10×18×6 foot storeroom?

4. Contestants on *Top Accountant* are each assigned a number, with each successive contestant's number being one higher than the last. If the producers call forward numbers 19 through 102, how many contestants are called?

5. If a six-year-old opera singer receives an average score of 4.1 from three judges, what score must she receive from the fourth judge to tie with a quadraplegic gymnast who got a 5.0 from all four judges?

6 In a non-rigged game of Spin the Bottle among seven contestants, one of whom is named Dolph Stallion, what is the probability that the bottle will land on Dolph the first and second spins, but not on the third?

7 If, after an elimination round, the ratio of members of the Zirconia tribe to members of the Yazoodle tribe is 7:2, and there are 27 contestants remaining, how many Yazoodles are left?

8 If *America's Pop Star* averaged 30 million nightly viewers a night over a six-day run, and *America's Favorite Embroiderers* averaged 2 million nightly viewers over its two-day run, what was the average nightly viewership for both shows?

9 If Sir Caviar can invite only four of nine bachelorettes on a group Jacuzzi date, how many different groups of contestants could he invite into the Jacuzzi?

10 If Jessica decides to date Adam, then afterward goes for Brady instead, then cheats on him with Chester before turning back to Adam and then leaving him for Brady and then cheating on him with Chester again, and the pattern continues, who will she be dating on the eightieth date?

11 If $l_1 \parallel l_2$, what is the value of m?

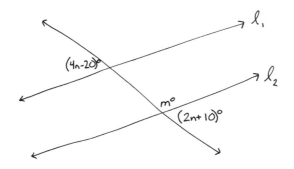

12 What does t equal?

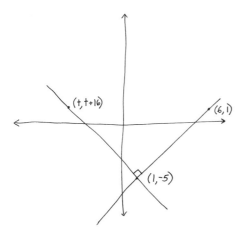

13 If the number of product placements on a show raises from 14 every 4 shows to 35 every 7 shows, what is the percent increase in average number of product placements per show?

14 If $x^{3/2} = y^{-1/4}$, what color is my shirt?

15 What is the area of an equilateral triangle with a perimeter of 18?

16 If a contestant flies to Hollywood at 900 mph and immediately flies back at 600 mph, what is her average speed?

17 If 40% of a show's 70 contestants are female, and 20 female contestants are added, what percent of the new show will be female?

18 If a team follows a race 40 miles from Xanadu to Farnbourne, and then 100 miles from Farnbourne to Ulin, and 25 more miles from Ulin to Juniper, and then returns to Xanadu by the most direct route possible, what is the difference between the maximum and minimum distances for the final leg of their trip?

19 What is the greatest non-positive even integer?

20 Jana says good-bye to her mother and heads off to an audition at 3:30 P.M. walking at 8 mph, but realizes at 4 P.M. that she forgot her head shot. If she calls her mom as she continues on her way, and her mom runs after her at 12 mph with the head shot, at what time will mother reach daughter?

21. If Buff Blond Guy #1, Buff Blond Guy #2, Token Minority, Blond Bombshell #1, and Blond Bombshell #2 are in a random drawing to see who will eat rodents first and who will eat rodents second, how many possibilities are there for the outcome?

22. According to the graph, what is the value of $f(f(0))$?

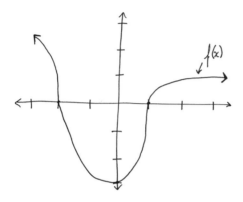

Critical Reading

Independent cinema, once known for nurturing critically acclaimed but unprofitable works, has recently produced works that are both respected and -----------.

   a. lucrative

   b. esteemed

   c. impoverished

   d. nonsensical

   e. artsy

2. It's no accident that good actresses keep choosing crappy roles; to the press they keep ----------- the ----------- of meaty characters, saying that interesting parts just aren't out there.

   a. bemoaning/lack

   b. whining about/incorrigibility

   c. disclaiming/accuracy

TRANQUIL: PEACEFUL

d. praising/absence

e. lamenting/surfeit

3. Any movie with Ben Stiller ----------.

a. sucks

b. rules

c. is a bomb

d. is a hit

e. is inconsequential

4. Though praised as a work of ---------- literature, the unconventional novel is unlikely to be adapted into a motion picture because of its lack of a ---------- narrative.

a. great/incoherent

b. erudite/burgeoning

c. abysmal/insightful

d. grueling/inferior

e. enthralling/cohesive

Questions 1–4 are based on the following passages.

Passage 1

The appeal of a violent film like *Apocalypto* is the deeply felt emotional response it produces. Slasher movies, war movies, and monster movies
5 succeed for the same reason—they are catharses for our deepest anxieties. Since he finds the prospect of violent death so alarming, a moviegoer can vicariously confront his apprehension, thereby
10 temporarily appeasing his anxiety. Films like *Apocalypto* are honest mirrors to a harsh word—senseless death *en masse* is a fixture of modern times, and obviously we as filmgoers seek out movies that
15 recognize this reality.

Passage 2

Over the course of *Braveheart, Passion of the Christ*, and *Apocalypto*, Mel Gibson the *auteur* has slain a good percentage of all the people who ever
20 lived. The question isn't whether his violent films are masterful craftsmanship (they are) or whether we want to watch the bloodbath (box office receipts say we do), but rather why they have found such
25 a niche. As I watched the onslaught of murders in *Apocalypto*, I began to wonder *who is anyone to wield this much power over life and death?* The buffer of the artistry wore away and the
30 horror began to chafe. I found myself dissociating from the death scenes, by the end feeling shock only if someone happened to die especially gruesomely.

1. The author of Passage 1 presents filmed representations of death as
    a. means to purge murderous feelings.
    b. mind-numbing ordeals.
    c. outlets for fear.
    d. vivid, skillfully executed representations.
    e. essential for a movie to be effective.

2. In line 30, "chafe" most nearly means
    a. scrape
    b. vex
    c. rub
    d. numb
    e. block

3. Both passages address which of the following topics?
    a. The financial success of gory films.
    b. The responsibilities of filmmakers.
    c. Why so many people like to watch violent movies.
    d. Emotional reaction to witnessing representations of death.
    e. How films reflect on trends in the rest of the world.

4. In comparison to Passage 2, the tone of Passage 1 is more
    a. anxious
    b. erudite
    c. conversational
    d. laudatory
    e. sarcastic

Grammar

Amazingly, rams' skulls have a substantial amount of elasticity, which allows them to survive <u>the fierce, powerful, and often brutal strikes of their competitors' horns.</u>

a. the fierce, powerful, and often brutal strikes of their competitors' horns

b. the brutal strikes of their competitors' horns

c. their competitors'

d. the fierce, powerful, and brutally placed strikes of their competitors' horns

e. the fiercely powerful and brutal strikes of their competitors' horns

what's with the morbid tone? sheesh.

It's tough to decide <u>who's horniest</u>, the great horned owl or the narwhal.

a. who's horniest

b. who is the horniest

c. who is the hornier

d. who's hornier

e. who of the two is horniest

3 With a body up to 110 feet in length, <u>the blue whale's central brain can't relay signals quickly enough</u> to its extremities, necessitating a smaller nervous center farther along the spinal column.

"Horny" meaning having big horns, of course.

a. the blue whale's central brain can't relay signals quickly enough

b. the blue whale's central brain can't relay signals quickly

c. the blue whale's brain, it can't relay signals at a fast enough rate

d. the blue whale is too large to relay signals, at a fast enough rate,

e. the blue whale can't relay signals quickly enough from its brain

4 <u>The offspring of a cat are much more numerous than an elephant.</u>

a. The offspring of a cat are much more numerous than an elephant.

b. The offspring of a cat, there are a lot more than an elephant.

c. Cats, they have many offspring, more even than an elephant.

d. The offspring of a cat are much more numerous than those of an elephant.

e. In the case of cats, there are more offspring than in the case of an elephant.

5 If anyone thinks an anteater is funny-looking, <u>they</u> should take a look at a multi-decked swarmy stinkerdoodle.

a. they

b. people

c. you

d. he

e. and they

TRITE/HACKNEYED: CLICHÉD

6 The <u>roving</u> band of yodeling dogs, <u>stampeding</u> elephants, and cooing
A   B
lions <u>are</u> terrorizing the local townfolk, who have already been
C
<u>thoroughly intimidated</u> by last year's hippo swarms. _____
D   E

7 My favorite part <u>of the movie</u> is <u>where</u> the gang of monkeys finally
A   B
makes <u>its</u> transatlantic voyage <u>to form</u> a new Monkey City in Tanzania.
C   D

_____
E

8 <u>Its</u> ability to grow fur <u>in order to</u> keep warm and repel water and its
A   B
capability <u>to produce</u> milk to better aid its offspring <u>defines</u> the platypus
C   D
as a mammal, even though its young hatch from eggs. _____
E

9 <u>A beaver</u> has more fur on one square inch of its pelt than a human has
A
on <u>its</u> whole body; the density of the beaver's fur allows it to trap air
B
near its skin, regulating its temperature even in a <u>frequent</u> <u>frigid</u>
C   D
aquatic environment. ____
E

10 <u>Although</u> the common bat has a prominent set of wings, no
A
contemporary scientist <u>had ever suggested</u> that <u>it</u> should belong to
B   C
Aves, the bird class in the scientific classification system first proposed
<u>by</u> Carolus Linnaeus. _____
D   E

11 Though humans are the only animals <u>that can legitimately be</u> blamed
A
for contributing to global warming, <u>they are</u> also certainly the only
B
animals to have a level of consciousness <u>high</u> enough to worry about
C
<u>their</u> environmental impact. _____
D   E

12 Jeremy asked if <u>I wanted</u> to go to the Hall of Mammals <u>at</u> the
A   B
American Museum of Natural History in New York City with Kate and
<u>he</u>, but I said no as <u>I had already gone</u> four Sundays in a row. _____
C   D   E

13 No one's really sure <u>whether</u> the cheetah or the tiger <u>has</u> better
A   B
prospects for long-term survival, but I know one thing for certain: <u>they</u>
C
sure are <u>faster</u>. _____
D   E

14 Although I recognize that she's a <u>world-renowned</u> biologist, <u>I</u> take
A   B
exception with Mary's constant distinction <u>between</u> "man" and
C
"creature"—humankind <u>are</u>, after all, an animal like any other.
D

_____
E

TURBULENT: VIOLENTLY MOVING

Drill Answers

Math

Answers	Page
1. 5	124
2. 33.75π	139
3. 40	148
4. 84	154
5. 7.7	96
6. 6/343	106
7. 6	108
8. 23 million	96
9. 126	101
10. Brady	121
11. 140	131
12. −11	143

(Remember: the slopes of perpendicular lines are reciprocals of each other.)

13. $\approx$ 42.9	110
14. White	119
15. 9$\sqrt{3}$	136
16. 720 mph	91
17. 53 1/3	112
18. 130	133
19. 0	152
20. 5 P.M.	91
21. 20	101
22. 0	99

Critical Reading Sentence Completion

Answers	*Page*
1. A	42
2. A	46
3. All are valid (though I suspect E is most appropriate.)	
4. E	46

Reading Passage

Answers	*Page*
1. C	50–64
2. B	64

(Remember: you're looking for literal, dictionary definitions—anything but "vex" works only metaphorically.)

3. D	50–64
4. D	50–64

Grammar

Answers	*Page*
1. B	181
2. D	193
3. E	188
4. D	189
5. D	187
6. C	186
7. B	191

UNDERSCORE: HIGHLIGHT

8.	D	186–7
9.	C	190
10.	B	189
11.	E	191
12.	C	192
13.	C	193
14.	D	191

The Day of the Test

Your Controlling Guidebook Boyfriend Tells You What to Eat, Study, and Wear

Look, baby, we gotta talk. I know you have your own sense of style and your own diet, and I love that about you, I really do . . . but you've already let me dictate your study preparations, so it's time you gave up control over your fashion and food, too.

The day of the test:

Dressing: Layers upon layers. Even if you're taking the SAT in your own high school, you have no way of knowing how chilly or sweltering the room will be. Sure, you've spent three years there—but who knows what it's going to be like on Saturday morning, when the assistant janitor's in charge? Layers are the key to temperature control. So, even if it looks atrocious, wear a hoodie over that sweater vest. (As a bonus, if you bring layers you can more easily sneak in energy bars to eat during breaks.)

Be sure to include a calculator and pencils in your accessorizing. I can understand if you prefer mechanical pencils (they're great for the essay), but bring some dull regular ones, too, for bubbling in. You can fill bubbles much more quickly with a nice thick old-fashioned pencil.

Eating: This is one morning you get to be a total brat: Guilt-trip your parent into making you a nice breakfast. Tell Mom or Dad your future depends on bacon and eggs. Ask for that "part of a balanced breakfast" meal you see on TV commercials, the one that no one in

Who Can Take the SAT?

SAT registration is open to everyone. You don't have to be a high school student. Actually, you don't have to be a student at all.

If it would make you more comfortable, you could have your mom take the test alongside you. You could have your little sister, your big brother, your whole family, even your forty-year-old boyfriend take it with you, if it would make you feel better about the whole thing. (P.S. You're seventeen. Ditch the forty-year-old.)

the real world ever eats. Even down to the two eggs, orange juice *and* milk, and toast/cereal. Feel free to vary it, but stick to a mixture of proteins and carbs, which release energy at differing rates and will provide you with both short-term and long-term rushes.

Studying: It's too late to cram, so don't try; it'll just get you anxious. But that doesn't mean you should shut the books yet. While you're eating your perfect breakfast, I want you to do three grammar problems, three math problems, and three sentence completions, chosen randomly from this book or a practice test. What we're doing here is getting warmed up, so that when you arrive at the test center you'll already have been in SAT mode for an hour or two.

Just slog through the problems, and DO NOT check your answers. The point is the warm-up, not the learning, and no one wants to walk into the SAT having just missed something.

The Final Key to a 2400, OR The SAT Post-Party

The SAT takes place on a Saturday, which is (no coincidence) the best party night of the week. The test makers planned it this way, so students would find it easy to unwind immediately afterward.

At least, this is the argument you need to make to your parents.

VACUOUS/VAPID: EMPTY

Everyone knows the SAT is a big stress. Use the instant parental sympathy to your advantage with one of the following approaches:

1 Throw a blow-out party. It's to relieve stress, remember. OR
2 Get your parents to take you to lunch afterward, anywhere you want. You can share all your test woes, and eat your favorite ravioli, or what have you.

VENAL: SINFUL (VENEREAL DISEASE = DISEASE OF SIN)

BONUS:
Applying to Colleges!!

"Um, Dude, None of This Worked" (OR *What to Do if the SAT Just Doesn't Happen)*

No one likes to talk about it (particularly not guides like this, which all pretend you're going to get a 2400), but sometimes the SAT doesn't work out. No matter how much you prepare (or don't prepare), you may not get the scores that you wanted. Maybe you don't get scores that are very high at all.

Don't forget that you can retake the exam. But once time is running out, at some point you just have to face it.

The SAT tests a subset of mental skills, privileging logic and reasoning above all other intellectual virtues. But those aren't the only abilities that are important for college success. Far from it.

We all know the student who doesn't find schoolwork easy, and has to work really hard to get his assignments done. But he does them, and is still an A student, will continue to be so in college, and will go on to have a fine, dandy life. This kind of student sometimes doesn't do well on the SAT, no matter how hard he tries.

Whereas that smartass who never has to study to get his A's wanders into the SAT without preparing and walks away with a 2400.

If you're the first kind of student, the one who works hard but never found school particularly easy, and you're not scoring anywhere near what you want on the SAT, *consider the ACT* instead. It used to be exclusively for midwestern colleges, but those days are long gone. It's administered almost as often as the SAT, is accepted by all major colleges and universities, and *is much more straightforward.* Sure, you'll still have to do some reasoning, but you'll find the ACT resembles a final exam in a course more than the odd multicolored beast of the SAT.

Most of the question types from the SAT will show up on the ACT, by the way, so this book will be as useful for you in preparing. The ACT has an essay and four sections: Math, Reading, Science, and English (grammar). Scores on each section are out of 36, with a 31 roughly equivalent to a 700 on an SAT section, a 26 about a 600, and a 21 a 500. If you're considering taking the ACT, download a sample test from their Web site (act.org) and see how you score in comparison to the SAT.

Don't try to guess whether your prospective colleges would prefer you take the SAT or the ACT. Just pick the one that gives you the highest score.

If you wind up going with the ACT, keep the following in mind:

1. There is no guessing penalty, so don't leave anything blank.
2. You might not have to take as many, or any, SAT Subject Tests. Check the admissions literature from the schools you're applying to.
3. The ACT is stricter than the SAT about which calculators it permits (primarily to avoid graphing calculators with "solve" functions, like the TI-89). Which isn't to say you can't bring one, but bring a backup in case it's confiscated. Check their Web site for their calculator guidelines.

If the ACT isn't going to work out for you either, then you can consider applying to an SAT/ACT-optional school. An organization called FairTest, which seeks to stem the undue emphasis on standardized tests in college admissions, maintains a list of such schools: www.fairtest.org.

VERBOSE: WORDY

The Secret Way to Take the Test and Have No College Receive Your Score

The ACT has one massive benefit over the SAT: score choice. If you take three different ACTs, say, you can pick and choose which results to send to colleges. So if you bomb it a few times, no one has to know.

When you send your SAT scores to schools, however, you send all of your SAT and Subject Test results, no matter what.

But there is one sneaky way to get around this. It only works for your very last test.

Say you've taken your SAT and your Subject Tests, and are decently satisfied with the results. But you still think you can get your SAT or Subject Test score a little higher, so you decide to retake in your senior fall. Here's how you can take the test again, with no consequences:

1. Send all your scores to the colleges you're applying to, before you take the last test.
2. Take the SAT that one final time. When you register, you'll be given the option of having your scores automatically sent to colleges. Do not do this.
3. Wait three weeks for your scores to be available online.
4. If you like your results, have them rushed to the colleges.
5. If you don't like your results, do nothing. Colleges will never know you retook the test.

Ha!

Picking Schools and When to Apply to Them

Admissions guides and admissions counselors always repeat the same (admittedly helpful) information. Apply to your targets, reaches, and safeties. Highlight your best attributes and explain any gaps in your application using positive language. Blah blah.

In this section I'm going to give you the insider tips that I haven't seen elsewhere. It's by no means an exhaustive guide on how to apply to college; it's just a set of pointers you might not have considered.

You're in one of two situations: You either have a college counselor or you don't. If you go to a private school, or a wealthier public school, chances are it has someone on staff whose sole job is to help students get into college.

If you go to a less endowed public school, you just read that and said, "No way!" You public school kids might, like I did, have a guidance counselor in charge of four hundred kids, struggling to keep students from dropping out to work or raise a child, and who responds, when you tell her you are applying to Harvard, "Oh! That's in New York, right?"

But the truth is that you're not necessarily better off having a college counselor. You'll certainly have a lot more control over the process if you're not receiving direction from a school official. College counselors can often do more harm than good. You have to remember that they're employees, and just like any responsible employee they're making sure they do their jobs well. And their job isn't really to get you into college: It's to get the highest acceptance rates for the graduating class as a whole, and receive the fewest complaints.

This means that (and I've seen it time and time again) college counselors will discourage students from applying to schools they have only a small chance of getting into. If you only have a 20 percent chance of getting into Penn but an 80 percent chance of getting into Wisconsin, say, many college counselors will steer you toward Wisconsin, because there's an 80 percent chance of your having been satisfied with the whole process, instead of 20 percent. So *don't let your college counselor steer you too low*. There's really no harm in applying to plenty of reach schools. If you apply to six instead of three, maybe one of them will see your inner worth and let you in.

If you don't have a college counselor, then you have all the latitude in the world. Apply to as many places as you like. When it comes to college applications, more is more. Don't worry about causing too much work for teachers writing recommendation letters. Once they've written one, it's easy to cut and paste to generate another, so apply to as many schools as you can before admissions fees get prohibitive. Eight isn't going overboard.

Don't put too much weight into the peculiarities of a campus visit. I have plenty of students who come back from college visits and say they liked the buildings but the tour guide didn't wear deodorant, or the host seemed like a snob, or the dining hall conversation was dull. No school has a uniform student body. Don't let your impressions of a handful of people sour you on the whole institution. If you write off a college because the admissions officer was picking his nose, that doesn't count. If you write it off because you saw rats in four different rooms, that counts.

Financial aid offers aren't set in stone. When you get an acceptance letter that includes an offer of need-based financial aid, there's no harm in pushing for more. I have a friend whose father called the financial aid office every day for six weeks, saying his daughter probably couldn't attend unless they gave more money. They finally coughed up.

Likewise, when I got my admissions letters from two comparable universities, one financial aid offer was much lower than the other. I faxed the higher offer to the other school, with a note saying I wished I could attend, but I was offered more money at the first. They faxed back within a day—offering $12,000 more. At two "need-based" schools.

What to Mention (and Avoid) in the Application Essay

You know how annoying it is when one of your friends calls with a story she *just has* to tell you about Friday night, and when she finally gets into it, it actually turns out to be about how all these guys were hitting on her? Frequently she'll end it with "they were so psycho" or "they were so sketchy" to make it seem like more of a story instead of her just bragging about how attractive she is. (Note: Guys do this just as often; I just used the "she" pronoun because "they" is only used for plurals, not unknown genders. Natch.)

The same thing goes for the college essay. You're going to be tempted to make it into a brag fest. It's *supposed* to be a brag fest. But at the same time you can't make it seem that way.

Confused? That's okay. All I'm saying is that you shouldn't write about how you almost missed the deadline for the yearbook, but pulled it off anyway and so learned the value of determination. You shouldn't write about how you love acting so much that you take every chance to go to the performing arts library and read about restoration drama. You shouldn't write that you've always found pleasure in swiping at yellow balls, and never feel such peace as when you're on the tennis court, graphite under your feet and tennis racket in hand.

Why not? If you were the only person to write this kind of essay, then it would be perfect. It demonstrates how great you are, and makes you seem like the ideal student—no, even better, the ideal person.

Too bad everyone writes this kind of essay.

Face it. No one's *that* wonderful. Sure, you might have saved the day on the yearbook, but you also forgot to give the advertising department the right deadline. Sure, you might research restoration drama, but you only came in fourth in the district monologue competition. Sure, you might feel at peace playing tennis, but you like the couch even more and won't go out onto the court unless your mom withholds your car privileges.

Think about the paragraph you just read. Isn't it much more interesting than the goody-goody paragraph? And, despite your instincts to the contrary, it's important to include an awareness that you have areas you want to work on, along with your strengths. The fact that you include weaker areas makes your strengths seem all the more believable. Anyone can lie on an application essay. In order to prove that you're telling the truth about yourself, you have to be fully honest.

Think back to the friend who told you the story about how everyone was hitting on her. Now imagine another friend who went to the same party, and tells you how she was so preoccupied with her personal issues that she had nothing to say and felt like the most boring person there.

VISCOUS: THICK

You instantly are reminded that she's *not* boring (no boring person would have the confidence to admit that she felt that way), and immediately want to find out more about what's going on with her.

Admissions officers aren't saints, and they don't have the same patience your own mother would have reading your essay. Give them something to engage with. Be sure not to give yourself too many flaws, of course, and to make them minor or even vaguely positive. (For example, you could mention that you learned the value of writing your schedule into a planner later than your classmates, or that you've been so immersed in the Environmental Club's campaign that you came close to overlooking your own little sister's burgeoning interest in global warming. Don't admit you're lazy, or that you cheat, or that your toenails turned yellow in sophomore year.)

An essential rule of writing is to *show* how people are through actions, not just *tell* what they're like. You may judge yourself based on your ideals, but others judge you based on your actions. Don't say that Pete was anxious for his admissions letter to arrive. Say that he spent the afternoon continually glancing up from his book to the mailbox. Don't say you're conscientious and hard-working. Say you're always the one left to turn out the light and lock the door in the school newspaper's office.

Sticking a Bow on Yourself, or Self-Marketing for Seniors

This feels crass, I know, all this positioning of yourself. But just like when you're interviewing for jobs, you're going to have to pay as much attention to how you appear as to who you are. I'll leave it up to you to be the best you can be. I'm just here to make you *look* better.

As you compile your application and go through your interviews, keep a couple of things in mind:

Appear Positive

Don't say your school paper didn't ever have enough space for you to run the kinds of editorials you wanted. Don't say your French teacher has never been to France and taught you to speak with a thick Georgia accent (oops, I did that on my application). Don't say you would have been the cheerleading squad captain if your coach didn't have it in for you.

Do say you're looking forward to belonging to a school that has the resources for you to research your specific interests. Do say you like North Dakota's French department for its high percentage of native speakers on faculty (provided, of course, that's where you're applying). Do say your cheerleading coach was a total bitch . . . er, I mean, do say that you are eager to be part of a school with transparent procedures for electing team student leadership.

Have Some Empathy

Look. Teenagers are infamously narcissistic. (For that matter, most people are narcissistic—teenagers are just infamous for it.) Admissions officers are going to assume you're self-absorbed.

Do your best to refute it. In a limited sense, you can accomplish this by listing extracurriculars or travel experiences on your application. But even further, try to show that you can imagine what other people are thinking. At an alumni interview, you'll totally stand out if you ask even one pertinent question about the interviewer's own life, like wondering how her degree from X college influenced her own career. In your application essay, show that you can understand how some people could see archery as a quaint anachronism, and then go on to say why you enjoy the sport anyway. Don't write about your trip to Honduras and

VIVACIOUS: LIVELY

immediately say how fired up you were by the poverty you saw. Keep the "I" pronoun out of it for at least a few sentences—if you can concentrate on other people, it will show true empathy, which is the rarest virtue of them all.

Crisis? Nah

For some students, the admissions process just doesn't go well. You apply to the wrong set of schools, and your safety school turns out to have been a reach.

If you don't get into where you wanted to, don't panic. It may seem like you're the only person in the world to whom this has ever happened, but you're not.

If you have to go to a school you don't particularly like, remember that you can apply to transfer away during your freshman year. Once you transfer, you can spend your last three years in your own personal Eden. Or, you might very well realize that your last-choice school turns out to not have been bad after all.

VOLATILE: UNSTABLE

Final Words of Ineptitude (Formerly Known as Final Words of Wisdom)

Last-minute advice is invariably annoying. You're in the passenger seat of the car on the way to the SAT, trying not to puke, and your older brother turns down his Evanescence long enough to remind you not to forget any vocab words. So now you not only have to worry about your fragile mental state, but about how to get your lips to come together in a polite smile so that a fight won't start and make you feel even more unprepared as you pull into the parking lot. Bah.

I'm not going to give you a whole lot of advice here. What I will say is that, in my whole life, including college and everything after, *I never had a more stressful year than my junior year of high school*. I had more hours of homework than I ever had in college (promise), and then there was this test with massively high stakes thrown in on top. So cut yourself some slack. If you're snippy, if you cry at odd times, if you find it too hard (or all too easy) to sleep, don't think that the rest of your life will be this way. Just put your head down and get through these next few months. It's rough, but handling this current stress well will set you up for the future.

And remember: The SAT is offered multiple times, and colleges really mean it when they say they take the highest scores from multiple administrations. Everything's not riding on just one test. You can always retake. There, doesn't that feel better?

If you've been doing fine on your practice exams but are worried about bombing the real thing, put those fears aside. In my experience, students do slightly better on the real SAT than they did on their average practice test. If you've been preparing, your test-day nerves will sharpen your performance rather than knock you off track. Think about it—you're less likely to zone out on reading passages when you know your score will actually count.

Remember—the SAT is just a test, and you've got a fresh chance to knock it out of the park each time you sit down to it. But even if you don't nail the SAT, your parents and friends will still be around for you, you can eventually climb Mount Kilimanjaro, you can love and eat and drink and be merry. Go play with your dog and remember that he doesn't care what score you get. Unless your dog's name is Yale. Then he cares a lot.

Who are we kidding? Not doing as well as you want on the SAT would suck. It wouldn't be the end of the world, but it would suck. So think about giving this book another read.

Just don't start reading it all over *again* when you get to that last line a second time. If you did, you'd enter an eternal SAT prep loop, which could be the actual definition of hell.

I'm out of here.

You're going to do fine.

Sending you good vibes,

Spotted on the Job, Park Avenue at 71st Street:

Yorkie with leather booties. Year-round.

ACKNOWLEDGMENTS

Erin Moore, my editor, is justifiably famous in the publishing business. I'm grateful for her excellence.

Richard Pine, my agent, must be bored by how often I sing his praises.

Jade, our artist, drew some marvelous characters.

Thanks to everyone who read drafts.

GLOSSARY

ABIDE: TOLERATE

ACRIMONY: BITTERNESS

ADORN: DECORATE

AESTHETIC: RELATING TO BEAUTY

AGGRAVATE: WORSEN

ALLEVIATE: LESSEN

ALTRUISM: UNSELFISHNESS

AMALGAM: MIXTURE

AMORPHOUS: SHAPELESS

ANECDOTE: STORY

ARABLE: FERTILE

ARCANE: MYSTERIOUS

AUGMENT: INCREASE

AVID: INTENSE

BANAL: DULL

BELIE: CONTRADICT

BENEVOLENT: GOOD

BOORISH/BRUSQUE/IMPUDENT/CURT:
  RUDE

CAJOLE: COAX

CALLOW: IMMATURE

CANDID: FRANK

CAPRICIOUS: UNPREDICTABLE

CASTIGATE: SCOLD

CAUSTIC: CORROSIVE

CENSOR: EDIT

CHIMERICAL: FANCIFUL

CIRCUMLOCUTION: TALKING AROUND

CIRCUMVENT: GO AROUND
  (**CIRCUM**FERENCE = PERIMETER OF A CIRCLE)

COLLUDE: CONSPIRE

COMMEND: PRAISE

CONCILIATORY/PLACATING: APPEASING

CONCORD: AGREEMENT

CONFLAGRATION: FIRE

CONSENSUS: AGREEMENT

CONVIVIAL/AFFABLE/AMIABLE: FRIENDLY

CURMUDGEON: CRANKY PERSON

CURSORY: ON THE SURFACE

DEBASE: LOWER

DECOROUS: WELL-BEHAVED

DEFY: GO AGAINST

DELINEATE: DEFINE

DIDACTIC: EDUCATIONAL

DIFFIDENCE/INTROVERSION: SHYNESS

DILIGENT: HARDWORKING

DISCREET: TACTFUL

DISCRETE: SEPARATE

DISINGENUOUS: FAKE

DISINTERESTED: UNBIASED

DISSEMINATE: SPREAD

DISSOLUTION: COMING APART

DOGMATIC: RIGID

EBULLIENCE/EFFERVESCENCE: BUBBLINESS

ELOQUENT: WELL-SPOKEN

ELUCIDATE: CLARIFY

EMINENT/PROMINENT: WELL-KNOWN

EMPIRIC: FROM EXPERIENCE

ENFRANCHISE: GIVE VOTING RIGHTS

EQUANIMITY: POISE

EQUIVOCATE: MISLEAD

ERRONEOUS: WRONG

ERUDITE: BOOK-SMART

EXCRUCIATING: PAINFUL

EXONERATE: CLEAR OF BLAME

EXTEMPORANEOUS: SPUR-OF-THE-MOMENT

FACILE: EASY

FELICITY: HAPPINESS/ACCURACY

FORGERY: FAKERY

FRENETIC: FRANTIC

FUTILE: USELESS

GRATUITOUS: UNNECESSARY

HISTRIONIC: OVERDRAMATIC

HUBRIS: PRIDE

IMPARTIAL/NONPARTISAN: UNBIASED

IMPEDE: BLOCK

INADVERTENTLY: ACCIDENTALLY

INCISIVE: CUTTING

INDIGENT: POOR

INEFFABLE: INEXPRESSIBLE

INNOCUOUS: HARMLESS

INTEMPERATE: EXTREME

INTUITIVE: INSTINCTIVE

INUNDATE: FLOOD

INVECTIVE: INSULT

INVETERATE/CHRONIC: HABITUAL

IRREPROACHABLE: BLAMELESS

LAMENT: MOURN

LAUDATORY: PRAISING (APP*LAU*SE)

LICENTIOUS: LOOSE MORALS

LIVID: SUPER-MAD

LOATHE: HATE

LUMINOUS: BRIGHT

MALLEABLE/ELASTIC: CHANGEABLE

MELANCHOLY: SAD

MERCENARY: MONEY-MOTIVATED

MIRTHFUL: HAPPY

MUNDANE: ORDINARY

NONCHALANT: COOL

NOVEL: NEW

OBSEQUIOUS: BROWNNOSING

OBSTREPEROUS: HOSTILE

ORTHODOX: CONVENTIONAL

PALLIATIVE: SOOTHING

PERMEATE: FILL

PERPLEX: CONFUSE

PERVASIVE: WIDESPREAD

PETULANT: SULKY

POLARIZED: DIVIDED

POLEMICAL: CONTROVERSIAL

PORTEND: PREDICT

PRAGMATISM: PRACTICALITY

PRECLUDE: PREVENT

PREDILECTION: FONDNESS

PRELUDE: INTRODUCTION

PROVINCIAL: UNSOPHISTICATED

QUAGMIRE: SWAMP

QUALIFIED: RESTRICTED

QUELL: SQUASH

QUIESCENCE: GIVING IN

QUIXOTIC: IDEALISTIC

RANCOR: RESENTMENT

RECLUSE: LONER

REFUGE/SANCTUARY: SAFE PLACE

REMUNERATION: PAYMENT

REPUDIATE: DENY

REPUGNANCE: DISGUST

RETRACT: TAKE BACK

SALVO: ATTACK

SANGUINE: CHEERFUL

SCATHING: HARSH

SCRUPULOUS: MORAL

SEDATE: RELAXED

SERENE: TRANQUIL

SOLICIT: ASK

SUBSTANTIATE: VALIDATE

SULLEN: SULKY

SUPPLANT: TAKE OVER

TACTILE: RELATING TO TOUCH

TEDIUM: BORINGNESS

TEMPERATE: MODERATE

TEMPORIZE: DELAY

TENTATIVE: UNSURE

THWART: FRUSTRATE

TRANQUIL: PEACEFUL

TREPIDATION: FEAR

TRITE/HACKNEYED: CLICHÉD

TURBULENT: VIOLENTLY MOVING

UNDERMINE: DAMAGE

UNDERSCORE: HIGHLIGHT

UNEQUIVOCAL: DEFINITE

URBANE/COSMOPOLITAN: SOPHISTICATED

VACUOUS/VAPID: EMPTY

VENAL: SINFUL *(VENEREAL DISEASE = DISEASE OF SIN)*

VENERATE: WORSHIP

VERBOSE: WORDY

VEX/RILE: PISS OFF

VIGNETTE: SHORT SCENE

VINDICTIVE: VENGEFUL

VISCOUS: THICK

VITAL: FULL OF LIFE

VIVACIOUS: LIVELY

VOLATILE: UNSTABLE

ZEALOUS: HARD-CORE

INDEX